OUTLINE GRAMMAR

OF THE

SINGPHO LANGUAGE:

AS SPOKEN BY THE

SINGPHOS DOWANNIYAS AND OTHERS RESIDING
IN THE NEIGHBOURHOOD OF SADIYA

OUTLINE GRAMMAR

OF THE

SINGPHO LANGUAGE:

AS SPOKEN BY THE

SINGPHOS DOWANNIYAS AND OTHERS RESIDING IN THE NEIGHBOURHOOD OF SADIYA

J. F. NEEDHAM

GYAN

Published by

GYAN

Gyan Publishing House
5, Ansari Road
Daryaganj, New Delhi-110002
Phone: 011-47034999, 9811692060
E-mail: books@gyanbooks.com

Distribution Network
gyanbooks.com
India, USA, Canada, UK, Australia

ISBN: 978-93-6780-141-3 (HB)

First Published, 1886

2nd Impression 2024

Printed at: Gyan Press, Delhi.

OUTLINE GRAMMAR OF THE SINGPHO LANGUAGE
Author: J. F. NEEDHAM

OUTLINE GRAMMAR

OF THE

SINGPHO LANGUAGE

AS SPOKEN BY THE

Singphos, Dowanniyas, and others, residing in the neighbourhood of Sadiya.

WITH ILLUSTRATIVE SENTENCES, PHRASE-BOOK, AND VOCABULARY

By J. F. NEEDHAM,
ASSISTANT POLITICAL OFFICER, SADIYA.

SHILLONG:
PRINTED AT THE ASSAM SECRETARIAT PRESS.

1889.

PREFACE.

SINGPHO is a language which is somewhat widely spoken in the vicinity of Sadiya, not only by the Singphos proper residing on the Buri Dihing, Noa Dihing, and Tengapani, &c., but by not a few other castes likewise.

As far as I can ascertain, from a cursory examination of a Burmese grammar by A. Judson, it has no very* close affinity to Burmese, which is somewhat surprising, when it is considered what near neighbours the Singphos proper are to the Burmese. The Singphos, however, allege that they are immigrants from a country very far away from where they are now residing, and this fact may account for the difference between the two languages.

Being divided into numerous clans, a few noticeable distinctions in the use and pronunciation of certain words undoubtedly exists among them, but, for all practicable purposes, the Singpho language as spoken in these parts, may be regarded as one dialect.

The Khâkhû's† (as the more distant Singphos are termed) dialect is, I am informed, essentially different to the one treated in this work, though it has very many words in it exactly similar to the one spoken by the Hukong and Sadiya Singphos.

J. F. NEEDHAM,
Assistant Political Officer, Sadiya.

---

* The Singphos themselves declare that there is no similarity at all between the two languages.

† Khâkhû means *lit.* the head of a river. The term is not applied to the Hukong Valley Singphos, but to their kinsmen inhabiting the hills and country to the north-east of them.

OUTLINE SINGPHO GRAMMAR.

PART I.—ORTHOGRAPHY.

1. Vowels.

a—when not marked always short, as in comp*a*ny, or like the *u* in t*u*b, s*u*n, &c.

â—long, as in f*a*ther, f*a*r.

Note.—The language contains a *few* monosyllabic words, which are merely distinguishable from one another by variations in this vowel sound, *viz.* :—

Wâ = tooth.
Wâ = father.
Wâ = root of verb meaning go, or move from any place.
Wâ = pig.

In the 1st the *â* is very long, the voice resting on it.
" 2nd " like the *a* in f*a*ther.
" 3rd " like the short Italian *a* in such words as w*a*ft, st*a*ff.
" 4th " long, but the word is uttered sharply like an exclamation.

Khâ = bitter.
Khâ = debt, borrow.
Khâ = river.

In the first the â is very long, in the second a little shorter, while the third word is pronounced sharply, like an exclamation.

Then we have "ngâ" = buffalo, and "ngâ" root of verb to be. Both "â's" are the same, but the one in the first is longer than that in the second word, which must be uttered sharply.

Also "gâ" = crack, and "gâ" = language; "jâ" = hard, and "jâ" = gold ; "nâ" = ear, and "nâ" = taboo ; where the same differences in sound exist.

å—like the sound of *a* in b*a*ll, as kå′sî = hunger.

e—unmarked like the *e* in m*e*t, b*e*d, &c.

ê—like the *ey* in th*ey*, or the *ai* in aim.

i—unmarked like the *i* in p*i*n, *i*n, &c.

î—like the *i* in mach*i*ne.

Note.—As with *â*, so with this vowel there are a *few* words which are only distinguishable from one another by variations in its sound, *viz.*,—

{ Lî = heavy.
Lî = boat.
{ Pa'sî = cotton.
Pa'sî = comb.
{ Ka'tsî = cold.
Ka'tsî = small.

We might compare the sound of "lî" = heavy, to the *le* in *legion*, and that of "lî" = boat to the French word *lit* = bed. In "pa'sî" = cotton, and "ka'tsî" = cold, chilly, the *i* is *longer* than in the other two words ("pa'sî" = comb, and "katsî" = small).

o—unmarked like the *o* in n*o*t.
ô—like the long *o* in b*o*ne.
û*—like the long sound of *oo* in m*oo*n.

DIPHTHONGS.

au—like *ow* in *how*! as "grau" = superlative.
ai—like the *i* in shine; "ai" = one.
oi—like the *oi* in b*oi*l.
ui—like *ui* in the French word app*ui*; as "gui" = about, or the point of, "ta'gui" = inside.

2. CONSONANTS.

b—as in English.
c—only used in conjunction with *h* when the *ch* is pronounced like the *ch* in *chair*, as "chau'sû" = slowly.
d—like the Sanskrit द
g—hard, as in *g*un, as "ga'gâ" = different, "gâ" = language.
h—as in English.
j—as in *j*oy, "ga'jâ" = good.
k—as in *k*ing, or *c* in *c*ut.
kh—like Bengali খ, "khâ" = river.
l—as in English.
m—ditto, the suppressed sound of this letter is initial in a few words.

---

* A few words have *u* pronouned like the *u* in bull, but I have not deemed it necessary to mark it. The language, too, contains a few words with *u*, which are only distinguishable by variations in its sound, as "yû" = look, "yû" = descend, "yû" = leave alone, leave off, and "yû" = rat!

n—ditto, the suppressed sound of this letter is initial in a good many words.

ng—has the sound of *ng* in ki*ng*. It is initial in a few words; as "ngai" = I, "ngâ" = buffalo.

p—as in English.

ph—has more the sound of an aspirated *p* than its usual English sound *f*.

q—as in English; as "qui" = *about, on the point of.*

r—as in *run*.

s—like the *s* in *s*un (Bengali স). I believe, however, that all initial *s*'s and a good many others too in Singpho should have a *t* prefixed to them, and be pronounced *ts*. Singphos are often provokingly careless in the pronunciation of this letter, for instance, the word for *cold, chilly*, is pronounced ka'tsî ka'sî, or ka'chî. The difference between the pronunciation of chî and tsi is very marked, if each letter is plainly and properly pronounced, but if the pronunciation of either be defective they appear less unlike one another.

sh—like the *sh* in *sh*ut, or *si* in vi*si*on (Bengali শ).

t—like the *t* in *t*eeth (Bengali ত).

th—as in *th*ou, *th*ere (Bengali থ).

v—like *v* in *v*oice.

w—like *w* in *w*et. but this letter in the mouth of a Singpho often closely resembles sound of long *oo*, thus "wû" = fowl, is often pronounced *oo*.

y—as in English.

3. Accent.

The accented syllable in short words I have marked with the acute (′) accent, while in words having two accented sylla-ble I have used the double mark (″) for the main, and the single (′) for the secondary accent.

In addition to these, I have placed a hyphen between such syllables as have not been maked as above, in order to show where the modulations of the voice are required.

N.B.—Many words have the suppressed sound of *m* or *n* before them, *viz.*, "m'phû" = approximately, "u'*tâ*" = a house, "u'khong" = two. I have placed the apostrophe (') between the consonants, but only the smallest stress is required on such initial consonants. For instance, "n'ga-jâ′" = bad, not good, the accent is really on the *ja*, although the suppressed sound of *n* can be distinctly heard while the word is being uttered.

General Rules relating to Accent.

The stress of the voice rests on the penultimate syllable of a word:—

1.—Nouns.—Some of these are dissyllabic, as "nûm'shâ" = woman, female, "si'tâ" = moon, "ma'nâp" = dawn, &c., and the accent is generally on the first syllable, even though some of them may have a short vowel in the first and a long vowel in the second syllable, but when their case-endings are added the accent is shifted to the second syllable ; as—

nûm-shâ'fê = to a woman.
nûm-shâ'nâ = of a woman.

When the case-ending is a double one, as in the ablative "goi'nan" = from, the main accent rests on the "goi," and the secondary one on the second syllable of the noun; as—

nûm-shâ'goi"nau = from a woman.

2. Adjectives—Such as begin with *ga*, carry the accent on the second syllable ; as "ga-jâ'" = good, "ga-bâ'" = great, &c.

3.—Verbs.—Root verbs of one syllable retain the accent on that syllable throughout the present and past indicative, and the future tenses, that is, so long as the tense suffixes are words of one syllable; but when, as with the perfect indicative a dissyllabic tense suffix is used, the accent is transferred to the first syllable of the tense suffix ; as—

sâ-hâ'dai = I have been.

Compound verbs carry the accent on the second root, as—

bai-lû' = recover.
bai-wâ' = return.
dî-ngût' = able to do.

When the tense suffixes are added, the main accent rests on the tense suffix if monosyllabic, and on the first syllable if dissyllabic, as—

bai-wâ'hâ" = (I) returned.
bai-wâ'hâ"dai = has "

In the imperative mood the accent rests on the root of the verb ; as—

sâ'û = go.
dûp'û = beat.

and the rule holds good with compound verbs ; as—

bai-wâ′û = return.

When the infinitive of purpose (a′jo*) is added to a verb, the main accent rests on the "jo"; as—

dûp′a-jo″ = to beat.
phûng-lip′ajo″ = to dive.

and in interrogative sentences the main accent rests on the particles denoting interrogation, *vide* page 45 *post*.

On the prohibitive particles "phûng" and "khûm" a slight stress of the voice is required, as on the *not* in the English sentence, do *not* go.

PART II.—ACCIDENCE.

I.—Nouns.

1. Gender.

1. The genders are two only, masculine and feminine, inanimate nouns having no formal distinction of gender.

2. Gender in the case of individuals of the human family is denoted by (*a*) different words; (*b*) prefixing the word lâ′shâ=male (human being) for the masculine, and "nûm′shâ" =female (human being) for the feminine, to the noun; (*c*) the affixes "wâ"†=male, and "jan"= female ; as—

(*a*)—*Examples.*

Masculine.	*Feminine.*
Wâ = father.	Nû = mother.
Châ *or* tsâ = father-in-law.	Moi= mother-in-law.
Chî=grandfather.	Dui=grandmother.
Wâ′dî=paternal uncle.	Moi=paternal aunt.
Châ=maternal do.	Nûdoi=maternal aunt.
Krî=son-in-law.	Nâm=daughter-in-law.
Ding′lâ=old man.	Gûm′gai=old woman.
Sa′brâng=young man.	Mû′khon=young woman.

(*b*)—Examples.

Lâ′shâ mâng or —— shâ. =son (*lit.* male child).	Nûm′shâ mâng or —— shâ. =daughter (*lit.* female child).
Lâ′shâ mi′yam=slave.	Nûm′shâ mi′yam=slave.
Lâ′shâ phû (*a*) or nau=brother	Nûm′shâ phû‡ or nau=sister.

* The *a* is merely euphonic.

† Wâ is also used (1) as a sort of *expletive* with neuter nouns, (2) as a demonstrative pronoun, equivalent to the English neuter pronoun "it," *vide* page 68 *post*.

‡ "Phû" means eldest brother or sister, "nau" youngest brother or sister. *Vide* vocabulary for explanation.

(c)—EXAMPLES.

Masculine.	*Feminine.*
Nûm'dû wâ=master.	Nûmdû jan=mistress.
Lâ'dâ wâ=widower.	Nûmdâ jan=widow.
Sing'phô wâ=person, male.	Sing'phô jan=person, female.
Mi'yam wâ=slave, male.	Mi'yam jan=slave, female.
La-gû'da"wâ*=thief, male.	La-gû'da"jan=thief, female.

The question "is it a male or female?" (human being) would be—

lâ'shâ kûn nûm'shâ ?
male or female ?

3. In the case of the inferior animals, gender is distinguished by the suffix "lâ" for the masculine and "vî"† for the feminine with the reduplication of the noun if monosyllabic, or of the last syllable of it if disyllabic; as—

EXAMPLES.

Masculine.		*Feminine.*
Gui=dog	..........gui gui lâ.	Gui gui vî.
Woi=monkey	......woi woi lâ	Woi woi vî.
Wâ=pig	...........wâ wâ lâ.	Wâ wâ vî.
Chap=bear	.... chap chap lâ.	Chap chap vî.
Dûn=rhinoceros	...dûn dûn lâ.	Dûn dûn vî.
Ngâ=buffalo	....ngâ ngâ lâ.	Ngâ ngâ vî.
Mo'gui=elephant	.. mo'gui gui lâ.	Mo'gui gui vî.
Shî'rông=tiger	.. shî'rông rông lâ.	Shî'rông rông vî.
Ken'sû=cow	..... ken'sû sû lâ.	Ken'sû sû vî.

Is it a male or female (animal)? would be—

Lâ kûn vî ?
Male or female ?

4. Gender in the case of birds (feathered tribe generally) is distinguished by the suffix "râng," or "lâ" for the masculine, and "vî" or "wî" for the feminine, with the reduplication of the generic term "wû"=bird, or the last syllable of the name of the particular bird referred to; as—

EXAMPLES.

Masculine.		*Feminine.*
Wû=bird (generally)	..wû wû râng *or* lâ.	Wû wû'wî.
Wû tông=peacock	....wû tông wû râng *or* lâ.	Wû'tông wû'wî.
Wû gê=parrot	........wû gê wûrâng *or* lâ.	Wû'gê wû'wî.
Kai'pet=duck	.........kai'pet petrâng *or* lâ.	Kai'pet pet wî.
Khô'khâ=crow	..........khô'khâ *or* lâ râng.	Khô'khâ khâ wî.

* "La'gû"=root of verb "steal' with participial suffix "dai," shortened to "da" for sake of euphony "la-gû'dai"=verbal noun, hence "la-gû'da"wâ"=stealing man.

† Sometimes pronounced "wî."

2. Number.

Where no ambiguity is likely to occur, the plural is not specially marked. When it is required to be indicated, the following suffixes are used, *viz.*, "nî,"* "bok," "theng," or "yông," &c., meaning heap, crowd, company.

EXAMPLES.

Khâ-mân'nî* jam'ram krit'dai.† Mishmis very afraid are.	Mishmis are great cowards.
N'dai m'bâ'nî ga'grî‡ kâp'dai. These cloths dirty are.	These cloths are dirty.
N'dai kû'wâ bok phâ mang§ n'khô'â. These bamboos any thing not worth.	These bamboos are useless
N'dai sing'pho theng lo kûn n'lo? These persons suffice or not suffice?	Will this many persons suffice or not?
N'tâ yông yông. Houses all.	All the houses.

3. Case.

The nominative, possessive, and dative appear to have genuine case-endings, though they are occasionally omitted, probable owing to carelessness, while the ablative, locative, and instrumental cases are formed by post-positive particles.

2. The nominative affix is î. It denotes the agent or subject of the verb, and is consequently often used to mark the *instrumental* case.

EXAMPLES.

Chap'î ngai'fê ma-khri'hâ. Bear me clawed.	A bear clawed me.
Gui'î ngai'fê wâ'hâ. Dog me bit.	A dog bit me.
Sing-pho'î khî-nî'nâ cha'rû gi-ning'dî Singphos their *mod* how tsî-jo'dai? make?	How do Singphos make their liquor?
Ma-nâ'î¶ m'bûng'î phûn n'khong Last night wind trees two ga-dông'hâ. felled.	The wind felled two trees last night.

---

* "Nî" is used to form the plural of the personal pronouns.

† "Krit" is an adjective, meaning, timid, &c., with the substantive verb "dai" attached to it.

‡ "Ga'grî kâp" is a compound verb, meaning soiled.

§ "N'kho" means useless, unserviceable; "phâ"=something so that "phâ mang n'kho'â" means, freely translated, utterly useless.

¶ This is the locative case post-position.

3. The possessive is known by the affix "nâ"; as—

EXAMPLES.

N'dai phûn'nâ n'khâ. This wooden cup.	This is a wooden cup.
N'dai do-mâ'nâ* ken'sû. This whose cow	Whose cow is this?
Ning-rû'nâ rê.† Ningru's verily.	It is Ningru's.
Gui'nâ ka'shâ khrû ngâ'dai. Dogs pups six are.	The dog has six pups.
N'dai ngai'nâ wâ'nâ si'nat. This my father's gun.	This is my father's gun.
Chap'nâ li'min ma'dai grau kûn tsî-rông'nâ Bear's claws sharp very or tigers li'min ma'dai grau'dai? claws sharp very are?	Which has the sharpest claws, a bear or a tiger?
Mân mûng Sadiya'nâ pai'jân ma'gâ Burmese county Sadiya of south direction âng'dai. lies.	The Burmese country lies to the south of Sadiya.

Occasionally, where the genitive is as much a genitive of *quality* as of possession, the "nâ" is omitted; as—

EXAMPLES.

Ning'nau mûn. Cat hair.	Cat's hair.
Shi'rông li'min ma'dai. Tiger claws sharp.	Tiger's claws are sharp.

Possessive nouns, too, when used as adjectives, drop the "nâ"; as—

EXAMPLES.

Mo'gui kông pa'si dô'dai rê. Elephant tusk comb broken verily.	The ivory comb is broken.
Bâ'zâr Sing'pho bok. Bazar people.	The bazar people.

4. The dative affix is "fê," which answers to the Hindustani "kô," and, like it, is used for the accusative case also, as—

EXAMPLES.

Ngai'fê yâ'u. Me to give.	Give to me.
Mang'fê phûn lap shî'râ mo-gâp'û. Dead body leaves with cover.	Cover the dead body with leaves.
N'dai'fê ma-khai'mâ ngû'dai? This what call?	What (do you) call this?
N'dai sing-pho'fê nâng choi'â khâ? This man you know will?	Do you know this man?

* No interrogative particle required, as "da-mâ'nâ" sufficiently implies interrogation. *Vide* page 47 *post.*

† "Rê" is the affirmative particle, or verb. *Vide* page 27 *post.*

5. The ablative post-position is "nan" = *from*, to which the locative particle "goi" is often prefixed, apparently to express the sense *forth*, *from*, &c., as—

EXAMPLES.

Ngoi nam goi nan* lû'hâ. I jungle out from got.	I got it from the jungle.
Khî phûn goi nan* krathâ. He tree off from fell.	He fell from the tree.

6. The locative case postpositions are "goi" and "î," and they appear to be interchangeable; as—

EXAMPLES.

Khî n'tâ'goi (*or* n'tâ'î) ngâ'dai. He house at in is.	He is in the house.
Ma-nâp'î wû goi'dai. Dawn at cocks crow.	Cocks crow in the early morning (at dawn).
Ning-rim'î shan nam nan prû'dai. Dusk at deer jungle from emerge.	Deer emerge from the jungle at dusk.
Sing'pho ai'mâ khâ î krat'hâ. Man one river into fallen has	A man has fallen into the water.
N'gâ goi (*or* n'gâ'î) dau'û. Ground on place.	Put (it) on the ground.

The locative case may likewise be made by adding the particle "dê"† = *in the direction of* (Hindustani "ta'raf") to the noun; as—

EXAMPLE.

Ma'rêng dê nâng sâ-hâ'khâ"? Village locality you been have?	Have you been to the village?

The instrumental case postpositions are "sî'râ" (or "tsî'râ") or "da'pham"‡ = *with*, *by means of*, but, as already remarked (page 7 *ante*), the particle "î" is often used to mark this case; as—

EXAMPLES.

Shan phî ning'shî tsî'râ gô'û. Deer skin knife with strip of.	Skin the deer with a knife.
Ngai ning'rî sî'râ la'pû sathâ. I spear with snake killed.	I killed the snake with a spear.
Khî ma'rêng wan'î khât'hâ. He village fire by burnt.	He destroyed the village by fire.
M'bûng'î phûn n'không ga-dang'hâ. Wind by trees two fell.	Two trees were felled by the wind.

---

* **In both examples "nan" might be used *alone*.**

† "Dê" also means *locality*, *place*.

‡ "Da'pham" requires the particle "î," denoting the agent attached to it.

7. When a numeral, or an adjective is added to a noun to form one word, the inflective particles of the noun are put after the numeral, or adjective; as—

EXAMPLES.

Nûm′shâ mî-pai′fê da′lâ ai′mâ yâ′û. Woman blind to rupee one give.	Give the blind woman one rupee.
N′dai nûm-shâ′mâng* yon′na† ga-dê′na″ These girls both of which wa′nâ ‡n′nau ? your sister ?	Which of these two girls (is) your sister ?

Abstract nouns cannot be formed in Singpho.

II.—ADJECTIVES.

1. The Singpho language has no terminations to mark the degrees of comparison. The comparative degree is expressed (*a*) by the positive with the ablative postposition "nan" tacked on to the noun expressing the thing with which comparison is made; (*b*) by the positive with a noun (or pronoun) followed by the conjunction "n′lo" = *than*; (*c*) by repeating the positive and inserting "mang" = *and*, *also*, between the two words; as—

(*a*) EXAMPLE.

Gûm′râng nan ga′bâ. Horse from large.	Larger than a horse.

(*b*) EXAMPLES.

Gûm′râng n′lo ga′bâ. Horse than large.	Larger than a horse.
Kûm′phrông n′lo jâ ga-jâ′dai. Silver than gold good is.	Gold is better than silver.

(*c*) EXAMPLES.

Gûm′râng n′lo mo′gui, ga′bâ§ mang ga′bâ. Horse than elephant large and large.	An elephant is larger than a horse.
Ô′râ m′bâ n′lo n′dai m′bâ ning′nân That cloth than this cloth new mang ning′nân rê. and new verily.	This cloth is certainly newer than that (one).

---

* "Nûm′shâ mâng," *lit.* female child.

† "Yon" means *both*, so that "n′dai yon′nâ" would mean "of these two."

‡ The "n" is a sort of reflective particle.

§ This method of expressing the comparative degree is also used by the Assamese.

"Grau" meaning *very*, *exceedingly*, is also used to form the comparative degree; as—

EXAMPLES.

Bai'nam	n'lo	gûm'râng	ga'bâ	A horse is larger than a goat.
Goat	than	horse	large	
			grau'dai.	
			exceedingly is.	

I am not quite sure that the above does not mean that a horse is *very much* larger than a goat.

2. The superlative degree is made by adding "yông'a* n'lo" = all than, followed by "grau," to the noun expressing the thing with which comparison is made; as—

EXAMPLES.

Nâ'nâ	m'bâ	yông'a	n'lo	ga'jâ	Your cloth is the best of all.
Your	cloth	all	than	good	
				grau'dai.	
				exceedingly is.	
Gui ka'shâ	n'dai	yong'a	n'lo	ka'tsî	This puppy is the smallest of all.
Puppy	this	all	than	small	
				grau'dai.	
				exceeding is.	
Yông'a	n'lo	la pân'î	khî	ding'la	He is the oldest among (them) all.
all	than	amongst	he	old	
				gran'dai.	
				exceedingly is	

3. The following are irregular in the formation of the comparative and superlative degrees; as—

EXAMPLES.

Ka'shâ = young.	Yut—Younger, or youngest.
Ding'lâ = old.	Lât = older, or eldest.

4. The adjective, *as a rule*, *follows* the noun it qualifies; as—

EXAMPLES.

Khâ shûng'â†	= river deep.
Phun châ'â†	= tree high.
Nûm'shâ phrâ-phrû'â	= woman pretty.
Kû'wâ-ga-lûâ†	= bamboo long.
Sin'pho n'ga-jâ'â†	= person bad.
Sî'tâ ning'nân	= moon new.

* This *a* is merely euphonic.

† This is the future tense suffix, apparently used adjectively as well. The fact is there is no formal distinction between adjectives and verbs, each in its root form is indistinguishable from the others, the "â" may, therefore, be intended for the future tense, and "khâ shûng'â" meaning the river *will be* deep.

It may, however, *precede the noun it* qualifies; as—

Nûm'shâ mîyam	Female slave.
Lâ'shâ mî'yam	Male ,,
Nûm'shâ mâng	Female child.
Lâ'shâ mâng	Male ,,
Ga-jâ'dai sing'pho*	Good man.
That'dai* m'bâ	Thick cloth.
Ga-lû'dai* chang'wai	Long stick.
Phrâ-phrû'dai mâng*	Pretty child.

When predicated of the noun or used absolutely, the adjective invariably *follows* the noun it qualifies; as—

EXAMPLES.

Gîn phrông'dai rê‡ Snow white is verily	Snow is white.
Pa'lâng ai'mâ phrông'dai ga'lêng châng'dai. Coat one white is other black is.	One coat is white, the other black.
N'dai m'bâ ôr'â m'ba n'lo phâ grau'â‡. This cloth that cloth than thin very.	This cloth (is) thinner than that.
N'dai shan yet'â. This meat rotten.	This meat (is) rotten.

5. *Contrariety* in adjectives is occasionally expressed by the negative *prefix* particle "n;" as—

EXAMPLES.

Ngai'nâ mâng n'ma-chî'â.† My child not ill.	My child (is) well.
Mûng'nûn gâ n'la-jâ'â. Assamese language not difficult.	The Assamese language (is) easy.

5.—NUMERAL ADJECTIVES.

1. The numerals from 1 to 10 are—

Ai	1	Khrû	6
N'khong	2	Sin'it	7
Ma'sûm	3	Ma'sat	8
Ma'lî	4	Cha'khû	9
Ma'ngâ	5	Sî *or* tsi§	10

---

* These are participial constructions, the "dai" being equivalent to the relative pronouns in English, and other languages, and their correct rendering being—

The man *who* is good.
The cloth *that* is thick.
The stick ,, long.
The child ,, pretty.

† "Rê" is the affirmative particle, *vide* page 27, post.

‡ "Grau" means in a very great or high degree, and is the superlative suffix of the language.

§ Some Singphos pronounce it "shî."

After which the cardinals are repeated and compounded; as—

Tsî ai ...	11		Ma'lî tsî ...	40
Tsî n'khong ...	12		Ma'ngâ tsî ...	50
Tsî ma'sûm ...	13		Khrû tsî ...	60
&c. &c.			&c. &c.	
Khûn ...	20		La'châ* ...	100
Khûn ai ...	21		N'khong châ ...	200
Khûn n'khong ...	22		Ma'sûm châ ...	300
&c. &c.			&c. &c.	
Dûm tsî ...	30		Hing ...	1,000
Dûm tsî ai ...	31		Hing tsî ...	10,000
Dûm tsî n'khong.	32			
&c. &c.				

2. To the numeral 1 the suffix "mâ" is usually added to denote a *single* one, but where in English the indefinite article would serve as well, the suffix "mâ" is often used alone; as—

EXAMPLES.

Sing'pho ai'mâ	One person.
Da'lâ aimâ............	One rupee.
La'tsâ† mâ	One (single) hundred.
Hing mâ	One (ditto) thousand.
Li-nî' mâ	One (ditto) day.
Li-nîng mâ...........	One (ditto) year.

This "mâ," may be, and often is, used with the remaining numerals, apparently to denote an *approximate* number; as—

EXAMPLES.

Kû'wâ khrû'mâ râ'dai Bamboos six about require	(I) want about six bamboos.
Ngai shan ma-sûm' mâ mû'hâ I deer three about saw	I saw about three deer.

These two sentences might be construed with "m'phû" which means approximately; as:—

Kû'wâ khrû m'phû râ'dai Bamboos six about require	(I) want about six bamboos.
Ngai shan ma'sûm m'phû mû'hâ I deer three about saw	I saw about three deer.

---

* Often pronounced "tsâ."

† "La-tsâ' mâ" does not mean 100 *only*, but merely 100. Singphos have a separate word for *only, viz.*, "chû" and 100 *only* would be "la'tsâ chû" or "la-tsâ' mâ chû."

3. Subtraction is effected by using the verb "râ" = *require*, and "dû" = *reach*, *arrive*, in conjunction with the infinitive of purpose "ajo"; as—

EXAMPLES.

N'khong râ tsî dû-a'*jo Two necessary ten reach to	Two less than ten.
Ma'ngâ râ dûm'tsî dû-a'*jo Five necessary thirty reach to	Five less than thirty.

4. Numeral particles are not found in Singpho.

5. The numeral generally *follows*, though it occasionally *precedes*, the noun it qualifies; as—

EXAMPLES.

Wû khrû Fowls six	Fowls six.
N'ta tsî mâ'sûm Houses thirteen	Houses thirteen.
Sing'pho ma'lî Persons four	Persons four.
Si'nat n'khong Guns two	Guns two.
Li-ning' mâ Year one	One year.
N'khong ning Two years	Two years.
Ma'sûm nâ Three nights	Three nights.
Cha'khû yâ Nine days	Nine days.
Khî li-nî' mâ ngâ' dai† He day a stayed	He stayed a day.
Ngai n'ta khrû mû'hâ I houses six saw	I saw six houses.
Wû tsî mâ'ngâ lû'hâ Fowls fifteen got	I got fifteen fowls.
Khî'nâ prât tsî ma'ngâ ming. Her age fifteen years.	She (is) fifteen years of age.
Sî'dai phûn ma'lî tsîdông châ'â. That tree forty cubits high.	That tree (is) forty cubits high.

6. A few words in combination with *numerals* lose their first syllables; as—

EXAMPLES.

Li'ning=year ... li-ning'mâ=a year.
n'khong ning=two years.
ma'sûm ning=three years.
ma'lî ning=four years.
&c. &c.

---

* This "a" is merely euphonic.

† Present tense used to denote past time *vide* page 31 *post*.

La'lâm=fathom ... { la-lâm'mâ=a fathom.
n'khong lâm=two fathoms.
ma'sûm lâm=three fathoms.
ma'lî lâm=four fathoms.
&c. &c.

La'dông=cubit ... { la-dông'mâ=a cubit.
n'khong dông=two cubits.
ma'sûm dông=three cubits.
ma'lî dông=four cubit.
&c. &c.

La'khâm=span ... { la-khâm'mâ=one span.
n'khong khâm=two spans.
ma'sûm khâm=three spans.
ma'likhâm=four spans.

The following examples will illustrate how these words are used in conversation in their abbreviated form:—

EXAMPLES.

Nyê mâng prât ma'lî ning dû'hâ. My child age four years reached.	My child is four years old.
N'dai lî ma-lî'lâm ngâ'dai. This boat four fathoms is.	This boat is four fathom (long).
Ngai'fê m'bâ ma'ngâ dong mo-dûn'û. Me cloth five cubit show.	Show me a five cubit cloth.
Ô'râ chong'wai tsî'khâm ngâ'dai. That stick ten spans is.	That stick is ten spans.

7. The adverbial numeral once is "ga'lâng" to which the (numeral) suffix "mâ" alluded to at page 13 *ante*, is added, and the remainder are made by cutting off the first syllable ("ga") and prefixing the numerals "n'khong," "ma'sûm," &c., &c., to the last syllable, "lâng"; as—

Ga-lâng'mâ=once.
N'khong lâng=twice.
Ma'sûm lâng=thrice.
Ma'lî lâng=four times.

Nâ'nâ si'nat ga-dê'lâng gâp'hâ?* Your gun how many times fired?	How many times did you fire your gun?
Ngai ma-lî'lâng gâp'hâ. I four times fired.	I fired four times.

* No interrogative particle is used, because interrogation is implied by "ga-dê'lâng," *vide* page 47, *post*.

Ordinals.

There are no ordinals in Singpho. Their place is usually supplied by a participle.

EXAMPLES.

Dai'nî ma-nâp'î ngai shan n'khong'lâng To-day morning in I deer twice gàp'hâ sing-oi'î gâp'dai (*or* gâp-da'wâ*) fired first at shot shan n'krâ'hâ n'thom'nâ gâp-da'wâ shan deer not hit next shot deer krâ'dî sî'hâ. hitting died.	I fired two shots at a deer this morning. The first shot I missed (but) the second hit (it and) killed (it).
Ngai sâ'dai si-nî'î nâp'shûr ma-rêng'î I going day on Napshur village at dû'hâ n'thom'î si-nî'î ma'râng thû'hâ arrived next to day on rain fell dai n'thom'î n'khong yâ mang subsequently on two days also ma'râng thû'hâ. rain fell.	On the first day I reached Napshur village, (and) on the second day it rained, on the third and fourth days also it rained.

III.—PRONOUNS.

1. There are three kinds of pronouns in Singpho, *viz.*, personal, interrogative, and adjective.

There are no relative pronouns, but their place is supplied by a participle.

6.—PERSONAL PRONOUNS.

Singular.

Nom.	Ngai = I.	Nâng = You.	Khî = He.
Dat. & Acct.	Ngai'fê = to me, me.	Nâng'fê = to you, you.	Khî'fê = to him, him.
Poss.	Ngai'nâ† nye'nâ, or nyê. = of me, mine.	Nâ'nâ† = of you. Nâ = Your.	Khî'nâ* = of him, his.
Abl.	Ngai'nan *or* goi'nan. = from me.	Nâng'nan, *or* goin'nan. = from you.	Khî'nan, *or* goi'nan. from him.

---

* "Gâp"=root of verb to shoot, "da"=past participle "dai," shortened for sake of euphony, "wâ" used as a demonstrative particle, so that "gâp-da'wâ"=shot that.

† "Nâ" is often pronounced "na" Occasionally the "n" is dropped altogether, as "khî â mâng" = his child, instead of "khî'na mâng."

N.B.—There being no passive voice in Singpho, the case of the agent cannot be expressed:

Plural.

Nom.	Î We.	Nî = You.	Khî'nî = They.
Dat. & Acct.	Î'fê = to us, us.	Nî'fê = to you, you.	Khî-nî'fê = to them, them.
Poss.	Î'nâ* = of us, ours.	Nî'nâ *= of you, your.	Khî-nî'nâ* of = them.
Abl.	Î'nan = from us. goi'nan.	Nî'nan = from you. goi'nan.	Khî-nî'nan = from goi'nan. them.

2. For the plural of these pronouns "yông" = all, is used; as—

EXAMPLES.

N'dai lâ'hû nî yông a' jò. This liquor you all for.	This liquor (is) for you all.
Î yông mû'hâ. We all saw.	We all saw (it).
Nî yông sâ-hâ'î?† You all go did?	Did you all go?
Khî'nî yông'fê lâ'hû jô'û. They all to liquor give.	Give them all liquor.
Nî yông khûn'khân rê. You all lazy verily.	You are all lazy.

3. The reflective pronoun is "ting'nâng," and is thus declined; as—

SINGULAR AND PLURAL.

Nom.	Ting'nâng...............	self, selves.
Dat. & Acct.	Ting-nâng'fê............	to do.
Poss.	Ting-nâ'nâ	of do.
Abl.	Ting-nân'nan goi'nan	from do.

EXAMPLES.

Illustrating how used.

Ngai ting'nâng dî'gâ. I self do will.	I will do it myself.
Khî ting'nâng sâ'hâ. He self went.	He went himself.
Ngai ting-nâ'nâ nan'fê yâ'hâ. I my own brother to gave.	I gave it to my own brother.
Khî ting-nâ'nâ nau-goi'nan lû'hâ. He his own brother from got.	He got it from his own brother.

* "Nâ" is often pronounced "na." Occasionally the "n" is dropped altogether, as "khî â mâng" = his child, instead of "khî'nâ mâng."

N.B.—There being no passive voice in Singpho, the case of the agent cannot be expressed.

† "Î" interrogate particle.

The last sentence aptly exemplifies the use of this pronoun. If the possessive of the personal pronoun "khî" were used, it might give another sense, as " khî khî'nâ nau-goi'nan lû'hâ" might mean " he got it *not* from his *own* brother, but from the brother of another person."

4. There is no neuter pronoun, answering to the English third person neuter pronoun *it* in Singpho. Occasionally, however, the third person singular of the personal pronouns is used to express it, as—

Khî'nâ tsi'râ ga-dê'goi? Its place where?	Where is its place?

7.—Relative Pronouns.

1, As already stated, there are no relative pronouns in Singpho. The following examples will illustrate how relative clauses are constructed:—

Examples.

Ngai kûm'phrông yâ'dai Sing'pho. I money given person.	The man *to whom* I gave money.
Ngai si'nat lâ-da'wâ* nan. I gun took man from. *or* Ngai si'nat lâ'dai* Sing-pho'wâ nan I gun or took person from	The man *from whom* I took the gun.
Ning-dim'î sâ'dai* Sing'pho. Last came man.	The man *who* came last.
Ma-nâ'î khât'dai* n'tâ'wâ. Last evening burnt house.	The house *that* was burnt.
Ken'sû si'dai* nûm-dû'wâ. Cow died owner.	The man *whose* cow died.

2. Sometimes a verbal noun is used to form a relative clause ; as—

Examples.

Nâ'nâ shong-phai'î ngâ'dai yông yâ'û. Your basket in existing all give.	Give (me) *what* is in you basket.

3. Or two simple predications are made, though this latter construction is rarely used ; as—

Examples.

Ngai Sing'pho ai'mâ mû'hâ n'dai khî I man one saw this he rê (or n'dai rê). verily.	I saw a man, this is he verily. (This is the man whom I saw).

---

* This participle ("dai") connects the verb with the noun, and is equivalent to our relative pronoun.

4. Relative clauses may likewise be construed by using the *interrogative* and *indefinite* pronouns in conjunction with the participle in "dî" and "mang"=even ; as—

EXAMPLES.

Ga'dai* mâng'î† ma-sû'dî mang sî-dai' What boy lying even that (boy fê dûp râ. understood) beat necessary,	The boy *that* has told a lie must be beaten (*whatever boy*).
Bâ-zâr'goi ma'khai ma'khai wû ga'jâ ga'jâ Bazar in what what fowls good good ngâ'dî mang lâ'û. being even bring.	Bring from the bázár what good fowls there may be.

Relative clauses of time, places, and manner.

The following illustrations will illustrate how these are turned in Singpho :—

EXAMPLES.

Nâng thô'goi sâ-yâng'î‡ khî'fê sâ You there going on him come ngû'dî§ sû'û. tell.	*When* you go there, tell him to come.
Nâ'nâ ma'rêng ga-dê'goi ngâ ngai'fê Your village where is me mo-dûn'û. show.	Show me *where* your village is.
Ga'loi¶ ga'loi yâng shan mû'yâng ngai Whenever deer seeing I gâp'dai. shoot.	*Whenever* (I) see a deer, I shoot it.
Ma'râng thû'yâng wat ngâ'dai. Rain falls when leeches exist.	*When* it rains, leeches appear.
Nâng ga-dê'goi‖ sâ'dî mang khâ You where going even water lû'â. find will.	You will find water *wherever* you go.
Nâng gi-ning'dî** dî'dî mang You how doing even n'ga-jâ'â. not good will be.	*However* you do it, it will not be well.

---

* Ga'dai mang = whatever.

† "Î" Nominative particle denoting agent.

‡ Sâ-yâng'î = root verb sâ = "go with" adverbial particles "yâng" and locative postposition "i".

§ Ngû'dî sû'û = compound verb, the first with participial "dî" and the second with imperative proper affix "û".

¶ Ga'loi ga'loi yâng = *lit.* when when being.

‖ Ga-dî'goi mang = wherever.

** Gi-ning'dî mang = however.

8.—Interrogative Pronouns.

Da'mâ ?= who ? It is thus declined :—

Singular and Plural.

Nom.	Da'ma ? da-mâ'î?*	Who ?
Dat. & Acct.	Da-mâ'fê ?	to whom ? whom ?
Poss.	Da-mâ'nâ ?	of whom ? whose ?
Abl.	Da-mâ'nan ? .... Goi'nan ?	from whom ?

Examples.

(Illustrating how used.)

Nâng da'mâ ? You who ?	Who (are) you ?
Nâng'fê da-mâ'î† dûp'hâ ? You who struck ?	Who struck you ?
Nâng da-mâ'fê mû'hâ ? You whom saw ?	Whom did you see ?
Nâng da-mâ'nâ gâ sû'dai ? You whose words speak (of) ?	Of whom do you speak ?
Khî da-mâ'goi"nan lû'hâ ? He whom from got ?	From whom did you get it.
Ma'khai ? = what ? Ga-dê'na"wâ ? = which ?	*Not* declined.

To the first (ma'khai ?) the particle "mâ," denoting *uncertainty*, is often attached ; as—

Examples.

Nâng'fê ma-khai'mâ râ? ‡ You to what necessary ?	What do you want ?
Ga-dê'na"wâ nâng lâ-a'î ? Which you take will ?	Which will you take ?

---

* "Î" indicating agent.

† Nominatival "î" denoting agent.

‡ Bare root of verb used, *vide* page 31 *post*.

"Gi'ning," in conjunction with the substantive verb "rai," is also used, apparently as an adjective pronoun, in the sense of *what sort*, or *kind of?* as :—

EXAMPLES.

N'dai gi'ning* rai'dai n'gû ? This what sort of rice?	What sort of rice is this ?
Nâng gi'ning* rai'dai mûng'lî dî ngût'â ? You what kind of work doable will be ?	What kind of work can you do ?

"Ga'dê," to which the particle "mâ," alluded to at page 20 *ante*, is usually attached = *how much? how many?* It is not declined.

EXAMPLES.—*Illustrating how used.*

Mo'gui ga'dê ngâ'dai ? Elephants how many are ?	How many elephants are there?
Nâng ga'dê ning nâng'goi ngâ'dai ? You how many years here dwelling ?	How many years have you dwelt here ?
Nâng-goi'nan nâ† ma'rêng ga-dê'mâ chân'dai ? Hence your village how far is ?	How far is your village from this ?
Sî-tâ'mâ"goi n'gû ga-dê'mâ shâ'mâ‡ ? Month a in rice how much eat?	How much rice do you eat in a month ?
Nâng shan da-dê'mâ mû'hâ ? You deer how many saw ?	How many deer did you see ?

Although "ga'dê" is not regularly declined, case-endings are occasionally tacked on to it; as—

EXAMPLE.

Phan ga-de'mâ"nâ n'gû nga'dai ? Kinds how many of rice exist ?	How many kinds of rice are there ?

"Kûn,§" a particle (answering to the Assamese "bâ" or the Miri "dî"), expressing *ambiguity*, is often tacked on to these pronouns; as—

EXAMPLES.

Da mâ'kûn sû'dai. Some one says.	Some one said (it).
Ma-khai'mâ"kûn dî râ ? Something do necessary ?	Something must be done?

Ga-loi'mê ? = when ? ga loi'nan ? = from what time or date ?

---

* Gi'ning rai'dai = (*lit.*) what being ?

† "Nâ" used for possessive case of personal pronoun, *vide* page 16, *ante*.

‡ This is the "mâ" alluded to at pages 13 and 20, *ante*; here we find it tacked on to a root verb as a sort of interrogative particle; "ga-dê'mâ shâ'mâ ?" means, of course, *about*, how much can you eat ?

§ This is the same "kûn" alluded to at page 46 *post*.

Examples.

Illustrating how used.

Nâng ga-loi'mê bai'wâ ? You when return ?	When will you return ?
Nâng n'dai m'bâ ga-loi'nan phûn'dai ? You this cloth when from wearing ?	Since when are you wearing this cloth ?

Adjective Pronouns.

The adjective pronouns are of three kinds, *viz.*, possessive, demonstrative, and indefinite.

Possessive.

The place of a regular *possessive* pronoun is usually supplied by the *possessive case* of the *personal* pronouns; as—

Examples.

Nyê mâng ma-chi'dai. My child ill is.	My child is ill.
I'nâ nûm'shâ n'ma-nau'dai. Our women not dance.	Our women don't dance.
Khî'nâ n'tâ gî-yûn'dai. His house leaks.	His house leaks.
Khî-nî'nâ â'gî nâng'goi ngâ'dai. Their headman here is.	Their headman is here.

My father, mother, sister, &c., are formed by simply placing the word father, mother, &c, after the genitive case of the pronoun; but for *your* father, mother, &c., the reflective particle "ning," and for *his* father, mother, the reflective particle ga" must be prefixed to the noun; as—

Nyê (*or* ngai' nâ) wâ. My father.	My father.
Ngai'nâ nû My mother	My mother.
Nâ (*or* nâ'nâ) ning'wâ. Your father.	Your father.
Nâ (*or* nâ'nâ) ning'nau. Your brother.	Your brother.
Khî'nâ ga'nû. His mother.	His mother.
Khî'nâ ga'nau. His brother.	His brother.

The *suppressed sound* of the letter "n" *prefixed* to the noun sometimes takes the place of "ning;" as—

Ga-dê'na"wâ nâ n'nau ? Which your sister ?	Which is your sister ?

9.—Demonstrative Pronouns.

The *demonstrative pronouns* are—

N'dai=*this* person, or thing, *near*.

Sĭ'dai=*that* person, or thing, *close by* or *in or out of sight*.

Ô'râ *or* ô-râ'wâ*=*that* person, or thing, *some distance off*, or *nearly out of sight*.

The plural is formed by suffixing the third person plural of the personal pronouns, as—

Sing'pho n'dai'nî. People these.	Those people.
Sing'pho sî-dai'nî. People those.	Those people.

Examples.

Illustrating how Demonstrative Pronouns are used.

N'dai mi'yam kha'mân rê.† This slave Mishmi verily.	This slave is a Mishmi.
Sĭ'dai m'bâ'wâ‡ noi'dî§ dau'û. That cloth hang up.	Hang up that cloth.
N'dai ngâ n'dai sing-pho'nâ"i ? This buffalo this man ?	Is this buffalo this man's.
Ô'râ sing-pho'fê ngai n'yâ‖ That person to I not give.	I did not give it to that man.

The particle "gâ" is sometimes added to these pronouns, for the sake of *emphasis* and *recognition*, as—

Examples.

Sing'pho n'dai'gâ n'ga-jâ'â. Man this bad.	This is a bad man.
M'bâ sî-dai'gâ jam'ram jê'dai rê. Cloth that much torn verily.	That cloth is much torn.
Phûn ô-râ'gâ ga-dâng'â. Tree that fall will.	That tree will fall.

10.—Indefinite Pronouns.

Da-mâ'ma"kûn *or* ga-dai'mâ"¶ kûn. ...	Anyone or some one.
Da-mâ' mang n'ngâ *or* ga-dai' mang n'ngâ.	No body (*lit.*) who even exists, not, *viz.*, "da'mâ" =who, "mang"= even, "n'ngâ"= exists not).
Phâ mang n'ngâ...	Nothing.

---

* More emphatic.

† "Rê=affirmative particle.

‡ "Wâ" is merely emphatic.

§ "Noi'dî dau'û"= compound verb, first "noi" root verb = hang up, with participial "dî" attached, second root verb "dau"= put, place with imperative proper suffix "û" attached.

‖ "N'yâ'hâ" would be more correct here.

¶ "Mâ"= numeral particle *one*.

Ai ai *or* kau kau	Some. This is the only way that this word can be expressed in Singpho. "Ai ai" means *lit.* one one and "kau"= half. These words are generally used in conjunction with the emphatic particle "gâ."
Jat, *or* yâ mang	More.
Lo lo	Many.
Made by using the interrogative pronoun "ga'dê"=how many? in conjunction with "mâ," the particle of ambiguity, and the participle in "dî" followed by "mang." *Vide* examples given *post.*	As much as, as many as.
Yông yông	All.
Made by attaching distributive particle "mê" to the noun.	Each.
Made by using interrogative pronouns in conjunction with participle in "dî" and "mang," *vide* examples given *post.*	Whatever, whoever, &c.

EXAMPLES.

Illustrating how Indefinite Pronouns are used.

Da-mâ'mâ"kûn ning-tsin'dai. Some one singing	*Some one* is singing.
Ga-dai'mâ"kûn prû-hâ'khâ"? Anyone come?	Has *any one* come?
Ga-dai'mâ"kûn n'dai m'bâ jê'hâ. Somebody this cloth torn.	*Somebody* has torn this cloth.

Here is another method of construing *someone* :—

Ga-dai' fê* rai'dî mang ai'mâ tsî-gâ'û. Whom being even one call.	Call *someone.*
N'tâ'î† da'mâ ngâ'dai? House in who is?	Who is in the house?
Ga-dai'mang n'ngâ. Nobody.	*Nobody.*
Ngai da-mâ'fê mang n'yâ. I anyone to even not give.	I will give it to *no one.*
Ga'dai mang n'choi'â. No one even not understand.	*No one* understands.
Ngai phâ'mang n'ngû'hâ. I something even not said.	I did not say *anything.*
Ngai phâ'mang n'râ. I anything not require even.	I require *nothing.*

---

* "Fê" accusative case, inflection.

† "Î" locative case, postposition.

Phâ'mang di phâ n'ngû. Anything even do like not is.	There is *nothing* more to be done.
Wâ ai ai gâ phûm'dai ai ai gâ la-sî 'dai. Pigs some fat are some thin are.	*Some* pigs are fat, some lean.
Mâng ai ai gâ nong nong krap'dai. Children some always crying.	*Some* children are always crying.
Ngai'fê jat yâ'î. Me more give.	Give me *more*.
Ngai'fê lo lo yâ'î. Me much give.	Give me *much*.
Ga-dê' mâ* mâ'dî. mang shâ'û. How much finishing (or consuming) even eat.	Eat *as much as* you can.
N'gû ga-dê'mâ lû ngût'dî mang lâ'û. Rice as much get able being even bring.	Bring *as much* rice *as* you can get.
Wû ga-dê'mâ mû'di mang† ma-rî'û. Fowls as many seeing even buy.	Buy *as many* fowls *as* you see.
Nâ'nâ kûm'phrông ga-dê'mâ ngâ'dî mang ngai 'fê yâ'û. Your rupees how many being even me to give.	Give me *as many* rupees *as* you have.
Ngâ yông yông sî'hâ. Buffaloes all died.	*All* the buffaloes died.
Wâ mang yông yông sî'â. Pigs also all die will.	The pigs also will *all* die.
Sing-pho'mê mûng'lî ga'gâ ga'gâ mo-dûn'û. Person each work separately show.	Show (me) *each* man's work separately.

11.—VERBS.

AUXILIARY VERBS.

Ngâ, Rai, Dai — All signify *to be*.

The latter ("dai") is, however, merely used as an auxiliary to "ngâ" and rai, and to other root verbs, to form a present tense.

"Ngâ" signifies *to be*, *to have*, *to possess*, *to exist*, *to remain*, &c.

---

* "Mâ" (pronounced sharply) means to finish, arrive at end of, so that, freely translated, the sentence means, eat your fill.

† "Ga-dî'mâ mû'dî mang" means, *lit.*, "how many seeing even."

The past tense is made by the suffix "hâ," and a perfect tense is formed by conjoining this particle ("hâ") with "dai," as—

EXAMPLES.

Khî nâng'goi ngâ'dai. He here is.	He is here.
Nyê khâ ngâ'dai. *Lit.* My debts exist.	I am in debt, (Assamese môr dhâr â'sê).
Lî'goi da'mâ ngâ'dai? Boat in who is?	Who is in the boat?
Khâ'î ngâ shan ngâ'dai. River in fish are.	There are fish in the river.
Ngai'nâ nau ngâ'dai. My brother is.	I have a brother.
Nâ'nâ ma-reng'î sin'pho ga dê'mâ ngâ'dai? Your village in persons how many are?	How many souls are there in your village?
N'dai ning'gûn ngâ'dai sing'pho. This strength possessing man,	This is a strong man (possessed of strength).
Ngai nâng'goi n'không ning ngâ-hâ'dai. I here two years lived have.	I have lived here for two years.

A past tense is sometimes formed by adding "ng" to "ngâ = ngâng" in lieu of "hâ," but "ngâng" is only used in the first person; as—

EXAMPLE.

Ngai ô-râ'goi ngâng'dai. I there was.	I was there.

"Ngâ" is sometimes compounded with a root verb to form a compound one, expressing a present act *not yet completed*; as—

EXAMPLE.

Khî yûp (*or* yûpdî) ngâ'dai. He sleeping is.	He is sleeping.

"Rai" also means *to be, to become*, &c. It appears to be used like the Assamese "hoi." The past and perfect tense suffixes are the same as those used with "ngâ."

EXAMPLE.

N'dai ken'sû rai'dai. This cow is.	This is a cow.
Khî moi* mî'yam rai'dai.† He formerly slave was.	He was formerly a slave.

---

* "Moi" means a long while ago.

† Present tense used to denote past time. *Vide* note under perfect tense, page 31 *post*. Here the word *formerly* sufficiently explains that past time is meant, and so Singpho usage prefers the present tense.

Tsi'phû rai'dî ngai n'lâ.* Rotten being I not take.	Being rotten, I will not take.

As with "nga," the first person singular of the past tense of this verb ("rai") may be made by adding "ng," but *for the sake of euphony*, the whole becomes "rêng"; as—

EXAMPLE.

Moi ngai mâng rêng'dai† yâ ding'lâ tai'hâ. Formerly I child was now old become (man).	I was once young, (but) now have become old.

Sometimes "ngâ" and "rai" are *compounded*; as—

EXAMPLE.

N'dai n'tâ'î wan khût phrin raî'dî‡ ngâ'dai. This house in smoke full, *lit.* being is.	This house is full of smoke.

Singphos have a separate verb for *become*, *viz.*, "tai" as—

EXAMPLE.

Illustrating how used.

Pa'gâ gâ'dî khî chî'thê tai-hâ'dai. Trading he rich become has.	He has become rich by trading.
Lam kûm'pâ tai'â. Road muddy become will.	The road will become muddy.
Nâ'nâ â-phî'âng tai'â. Your benefit become will.	It will be for your advantage (advantage will accrue).
Yâ khî'nâ tai'hâ. Now his become has.	It is now his.
Ngai ding'lâ tai'hâ. I old man become have.	I am become an old man.

"Rê," meaning *indeed verily*, is used as a verb of *certainty* or *affirmation*, something like the Bengali বট.

With the *suppressed sound* of "n" *prefixed*, it becomes a verb of *negation*, as—

EXAMPLES.

Khî Hûkong'nâ sing'pho rê. He Hukong of man verily.	He *is* a Hukong man.
N'dai ken'sû rê. This cow verily.	This *is* a cow.

---

* Here we have the bare root of the verb in its negative form, the future tense suffix being omitted.

† "Rai'hâ" would be quite as correct.

‡ "Rai'dî ngâ'dai," compound verb, the first with participal "dî" attached.

Khî ma'nâ phâ rê. He fool like verily.	He resembles a fool verily.
Dai'ni ma'râng thû'â rê. This day rain fall will verily.	It will indeed rain to-day.
Kû'wâ khrâng'dai rê. Bamboos hollow are verily.	Bamboos are hollow.
M'bâ n'dai ning'nân rê. Cloth this new verily.	This cloth (is) new.
Ngâ shan n'dai ka'shing n'rê. Fish this fresh not.	This fish (is) not fresh.
Khî chê'thê sing'pho n'rê. He rich man not.	He (is) not a rich man.
Teng'dai n'rê. True is not.	It (is) not true.
Ning'shin n'rê. Dark not.	It (is) not dark.
Dai'nî n'rê. This day not.	Not to-day.
Ma'ning n'rê. Last year not.	Not last year.
Rau n'rê. Together not.	Not together.
N'dai sat n'rê. This manner not.	Not in this manner.

Negation with the last five examples can only be made in the manner shown.

Sometimes "rê" is used interrogatively; as—

EXAMPLE.

N'dai si'nat da-ma'nâ rê ? This gun whose verily?	Whose gun is this?

This sentence might be equally correctly rendered thus—

EXAMPLES.

N'dai da-mâ'nâ si'nat ? This whose gun ? *or* si'nat n'dai dâ mâ'nâ Gun this whose ?	Whose gun is this ?

"Dai" in addition to being used as an auxiliary to "ngâ" and "rai," and to other root verbs, serves as a connective between the nominative and its qualifying adjective; as—

EXAMPLES.

Ô'râ sing'phô ga-lû'dai. That man tall is.	That man is tall.
N'lûng jâ'dai. Stone hard is.	Stone is hard.
Pâ'sî kyâ'dai. Cotton soft is.	Cotton is soft.
Nâ'nâ kan sau'dai. Your belly fat is.	Your belly is fat.

In *affirmative* sentences in the *present* tense "dai" is *usually* omitted after a noun, or adjective; as—

EXAMPLES.

Sî'dai sing'pho ngai'nâ gun'jâng. That person my enemy.	That person (is) my enemy.
N'dai nûm'shâ mû'khon. This woman young.	This woman (is) young.
Ngai ma'chî. I ill.	I (am) ill.
Khî ding'lâ. He old.	He (is) old.

Negation, with the substantive verbs "ngâ" and "rai" is expressed by the *suppressed sound* of the letter "n" put *before* the verb, "n'ngâ" means *does not exist*, or *is not to be found*, or *obtained*, whilst "n'rai" simply means *is not.*

EXAMPLES.

Khî nang'goi n'ngâ. He here not.	He is not here.
Khâ'î* ngâ shan n'ngâ. River in fish none.	There are no fish in the river.
N'dai nâ'nâ ken'sû n'rê *or* n'rai'dai. This your cow not is.	This is not your cow.
Ngai ding'lâ n'rai'dai (*or* n'rê). I old man not am.	I am not an old man.
Nyê khâ n'ngâ My debts exists.	I have no debts.
Nyê nau n'ngâ. My brother exist.	I have no brother.
Khî mî'yam n'rai'dai. He slave not is.	He is not a slave.

Sometimes "ka'tâ," meaning without, destitute of, is used in lieu of the negative substantive verb to denote negation, as—

EXAMPLE.

Nyê'nâ yâm ka'tâ. My powder none.	I have no power.

Root verbs are quite regular in their conjugation.

---

* "Î" locative case postposition.

CONJUGATIONAL EXAMPLES.

Verb "sa"=to pass from one place to another (go).*

INDICATIVE MOOD.

PRESENT TENSE.

The present tense is formed by adding "dai" to the root, but the mere root of the verb is often alone used to denote this tense.

Singular.		*Plural.*	
Ngai sâ'dai	= I go.	Î sâ'dai	= We go.
Nâng sâ'dai	= Thou goest.	Nî sâ'dai	= You go.
Khî sâ'dai	= He goes.	Khî'nî sâ'dai	= They go.

Present Definite.

The present definite is used to express a present act, or event which is not yet completed. It is made by compounding a (root verb) participle with the substantive verb "ngâ;" as—

EXAMPLES.

Khî shat shâ'dî ngâ'dai.
He rice eating is. } He is (now) eating.

Ma'râng thû'dî ngâ'dai.
Rain falling is. } It is still raining.

Sometimes the participial suffix "dî" is omitted; as—

EXAMPLES.

Khî yûp† ngâ'dai.
He sleeping. } He is sleeping.

Khi ma'nau yû ngâ'dai.
He dance looking at. } He is looking at the dancing.

PAST TENSE.

The past tense is made by adding "hâ" to the root; as—

Singular.	*Plural.*
Ngai sâ'hâ—I went.	Î sâ'hâ—We went.
Nâng sâ'hâ—Thou went.	Nî sâ'hâ—You went.
Khî sâhâ—He or she went.	Khînî sâ'hâ—They went.

EXAMPLE.

Ma'nî ngai khâ'man ma'sûm ka-tût'hâ.
Yesterday I Mishmis three met. } Yesterday I met three Mishmis.

---

* "Sâ" is used to denote motion to or from a person or place, so that it may mean *come* as well as *go*; as "nâ sâ"= *come* here; "dê'goi sa" = *go* there.

† "Yûp ngâ'dai" is used instead of "yûp'dî ngâ'dai."

PERFECT TENSE.

This tense is formed by combining the suffix "hâ," with the auxiliary "dai;" as—

Singular.	*Plural.*
Ngai sâ-hâ'dai—I have been	Î sâ-hâ'dai—We have been.
Nâng sâ-hâ'dai—Thou hast been	Nî sâ-hâ'dai—You have been.
Khî sâ-hâ'dai—He or she has been	Khî'nî sâ-hâ'dai—They have been.

EXAMPLE.

N'gâ gui wû ma'ngâ lâ-hâ'dai. Jackals fowls five taken have.	(The) jackals have taken five fowls.

N.B.—Singphos are wont to make but little distinction between *past* and *present* time. They constantly use the *present* tense when alluding to *past* time, especially when the time signified may be determined by some word in the sentence; as—

EXAMPLES.

Khî ma'nî ba-zâr'goi sâ'dai. He yesterday bazar to goes.	He went to the bázár yesterday.
Moi ngai mâng rai'dai. Formerly I child am.	I was once a child.

Again, the mere root of the verb is often used, without any tense suffixes, to denote *present*, *past*, and *future* time; as—

EXAMPLES.

Nâng'fê ma-khai'mâ râ? You what require?	What do you want?
Ngai ma'khai dî? I what do?	What shall I do?
La-châ'mâ ngâ. Hundred are	There are a hundred.
Ga-loi'mê nâng khî'fê mû? When you him see?	When did you see him?
Nâ'nâ mû'mûng ga-dê'mâ ngâ? Your mangoes how many are?	How many mangoes have you?
Khî ma-khai'mâ sû? He what say?	What did he say?
Nâng phâ mang n'dî. You nothing do.	You do nothing.
Dai'nî ngai n'sâ. To-day I not go.	I will not go to-day.

It will be observed that no interrogative particles are used in any of the above sentences, as each contains some word implying interrogation, *vide* page 47 *post*.

FUTURE TENSE.

The future tense is formed by the suffix "â," which may be used definitely or indefinitely as to future time; as—

Singular.	*Plural.*
Ngai sâ'â—I will go.	Î sâ'â—We will go.
Nâng sâ'â—You will go.	Nî sâ'â—You will go.
Khî sâ'â—He or she will go.	Khî'nî sâ'â—They will go.

EXAMPLES.

Khî nâng'goi sâ'â He hither come will.	He will come hither.
Jan m'pho'nî prû'â. Sun tomorrow rise will.	The sun will rise tomorrow.
Ngai khî'fê lêp'â I him overtake will.	I will overtake him.

The first person *singular* and *plural* of this tense may likewise be made by the suffix "gâ."

It (gâ) generally refers to a *near** future, and in some connections is hardly distinguishable from the present, thus "sâ'gâ" = I am going, the mind of the speaker having been made up, and he on the point of fulfilling his determination.

"Gâ" is used with the second and third persons of the imperative mood, apparently to express a *command*.

POTENTIAL MOOD.

When *power* or *capacity* is intended to be implied, the word "ngût" = *able*, is added to the root. As in Assamese, the future tense only is used, which, as already stated, is made by adding "â" to the root; as—

EXAMPLES.

Ngai pôn ngût'â. I lift able will.	I can lift it.
Ngai phûng'yot ngût â. I swim able will.	I can swim.
Nâng phûng'yot ngût'â î† ? You swim able will?	Can you swim?
Sing-pho'î yâm tsî'jô ngût'â khâ† ? Singphos powder make able will?	Can Singphos make powder?

---

* *Vide* ninth sentence, page 50 *post*, where "gâ" is used to denote a distant future!

† "Î" and "khâ" interrogative particles.

Negation is made by the *suppressed* sound of "n" before the "ngût;" as—

EXAMPLES.

Ngai pon n'ngût'â I lift unable will.	I cannot lift it.
Ngai phûng'yot n'ngût'â I swim unable will.	I cannot swim.

CONDITIONAL MOOD.

Conditional sentences are constructed by participial forms of the verb; as—

EXAMPLES.

Mâng dûp yâng'gâ krap'â. Child beating shall cry will.	If (I) beat the child, it will cry.
Khî sâ mî'yû yâng'gâ sâ ngû'û He go wishing shall go let.	If he wishes to go, let him.
Ngai shî'rông mû-yâng'gâ krit'gâ I tiger seeing shall fear shall.	If I see a tiger, I will be afraid.

"Yâng gâ" is used *indiscriminately* for the *present*, *past*, and *future* tenses.

N.B.—A past tense is occasionally made by using the past participle with "gâ"; as—

Ngai khî'fê mû-dî'gâ sû-â'mâ I him having seen tell will.	Had I seen him, I would have told him.

Sometimes an interrogative pronoun, or an adverb in conjunction with the indefinite past participle in "dî" of some root verb or of the substantive verb "rai," and the conjunction "mang" is used to construct a conditional clause; especially where in English the sentence begins with *whoever*, *whatever*, *wherever*, &c.; as—

EXAMPLES.

Ga-dai'mâ* rai'dî mang Whoever being even.	*Whoever* it may be.
Ga-dê'mâ chân'dî mang How far being even.	*However* far it may be.
Ga'dê ga-dê'goi sâ'dî mang ngai wat mû'dai. Wherever going even I leeches see.	*Wherever* I go, I see leeches.

* "î" nominatival "i" denoting *agent* of verb.

† Particle of ambiguity.

IMPERATIVE MOOD.

Sâ'û*	Go thou	(Imperative proper.)
Sâ sâ'gâ	Let us go	(Assamese "bol âmî jaun.")
Sâ-û'gâ.	Let him go	(ditto "hî jo'ûk.")

EXAMPLES.

Gî-vin'û .... Turn round.

Nâ ma'gâ yû'û.
This direction look. } Look in this direction,

Khî sâ-û'gâ.
He come let. } Let him come.

The first person singular and plural of the imperative is made by suffixing "î" for "û" to the root; as—

EXAMPLES.

Ngai'fê yâ'î.
Me give. } Give me.

Î'fê mo-dûn'î.
Us show. } Show us.

The prohibitive form is made by placing "khûm", or "phûng"=*don't*, *before*, the verb, in the imperative mood; as—

EXAMPLES.

Phûng sâ'û.
Don't go. } Don't go.

Phûng yûp'û.
Don't sleep. } Don't sleep.

Khî'fê khûm dûp'û.
Him don't beat. } Don't beat him.

INFINITIVE MOOD.

The mere root of the verb is usually used for the infinitive; as—

EXAMPLES.

Ma'nau† nau ai'dai.
Dance good is. } It is good to dance.

La'gû n'ai'dai.
Steal bad is. } It is bad to steal.

Dî la-jâ'dai
Do easy is. } It is easy to do.

Ngai mûng'lî dî n'ngût'â
I work do unable. } I am unable to do the work.

Nâng ma'nau yû sâ-dai'î?
You dance see going are? } Are you going to see the dancing?

* "Sâ'sû" is a common form of the imperative proper used possibly when it is intended to soften the command.

† "Ma'nau"=dance, noun, "ma'nau nau"=dance, verb. Here the noun is repeated in the verb.

Sâ-heb'î* gâp'dai shî'rong nâng Saheb shot tiger you yû sâ'hâ khâ? see been?	Have you been to see the tiger which the Saheb shot?
Ngai khî'fê ga'lau ga'lau sâ'û I him quickly go ngû'hâ. told.	I told him to go quickly.

In the latter sentence the Hindustani idiom is followed "main'nê ûs'sê kâ'hâ kî jal-dî jau," I said to him go quickly.

The infinitive *of purpose* is "a'jo†" added to the root of the verb; as—

EXAMPLES.

Khî lî yû-a'jo sâ'hâ ...	He has gone to see the boat.
N'dai n'khâ n'chin lû-a'jo ...	This cup is for the purpose of drinking.
Nâng mo-dûn'a'joi lâ'hâ. You show for to took.	He took it to show you.

Partiples.

Sâyâng..................	Going (adverbial and indefinite).
Sâ'dî	Having gone (perfect participle indefinite).
Sâ'dai	Gone (past passive).
Sâ-da'‡ wâ jan.........	Goes, one who goes.

EXAMPLES.

Illustrating how participles are used.

Dihong khâ rap'yâng Abor Dihong river crossing while Abor n'không sî'hâ. two died.	The Abors were drowned while crossing the Dihong.
Khî dû-yâng'î§ ngai sâ'gâ. He arriving on I go shall.	When he comes I will go.
Nâng yûp'dî‖ ngâ'yâng ma'râng You sleeping while rain shî'bâ krat'hâ. much fell.	Much rain fell while you were sleeping.

---

* "Î" nominatival, denoting agent.
† The "a" is merely euphonic.
‡ "Da"="dai", and shortened for sake of euphony.
§ "Î" locative case postposition.
‖ "Yûp'dî ngâ'yâng"=compound verb, *vide* page 30 *ante*.

"Yâng" is used in *all* cases in which *if* and *when* are used in English. When it is put *before* the nominative case, it indicates a *contingency;* as—

EXAMPLES.

Shan mû-yâng'gâ nâng'fê sû'gâ. Deer seeing shall you say shall.	If, or when I see a deer, I will tell you.
Shat* shâ-yâng' ngai sâ'gâ. Food eating I go shall.	I will go after I have eaten.

"I will tell you when I see a deer" and "I will eat and go" would be rendered—

Ngai shan mû'dî nâng'fê sû'gâ. I deer seeing you say shall.	I will tell you when I see a deer (*lit.*, having seen a deer will tell you).
Ngai fshat* shâ'dî sâ'gâ. I food eating go shall.	I will eat and go.

Past Participle Indefinite in "dî."

Khî sâ'dî yû'hâ. He gone having saw.	He went and saw.
Ngai shat* shâ'dî bai-wâ'gâ. I food eaten having return shall.	I will eat and return.
Shan ngai'fê mû'dî phrông'hâ. Deer me seen having fled.	The deer ran off on seeing me.
N'dai sat ngû'dî khî bai-wâ' hâ. This wise said having he returned.	Having thus spoken, he departed.
Mû'mûng tsî† lo lo shâ'dî Mangoes many eaten having ma'chî tai'hâ. ill became.	Having eaten many mangoes, he became ill.

If the conjunction "mang" = *even*, be *added* to this participle, it gives the idea of *although*, and is equivalent to having *though* at the beginning of the sentence, followed by *yet* in the latter part; as—

EXAMPLES.

Ngai shan krâ'dî mang phrông'ha. I deer hit having even fled.	Though I hit the deer, (yet) it ran away.
Ngai m'bâ lo-î'mâ phûn'dî mang I clothes few worn having even n'ka'. shûng"dai. not cold is.	Though I wear little clothes, (yet I) am not cold.

---

* "Shat" means, *lit.*, cooked rice, but appears to resemble our English word *food.*

† "Tsî" means fruit, Assamese "gû'tî."

The *continuance* of an act is expressed by *repeating* the participle. Sometimes "krai" is used for the first, and "dî" for the second participial suffix, as—

EXAMPLES.

Khî tam'krai tam'dî He search having search having ning-dim'î lûhâ. at last found.	Continuing to search, he at last found.
Khî khân'dî khân'dî He tracked having tracked having ning-dim'î shan lû'hâ. at last deer found.	He continuing to track the deer at last found (it).
N'khong yâ ma'râng thû'krai Two days rain fallen having thû'dî khâ tûng'hâ. fallen having river rose.	(The) rain continuing for two days, (the) river rose.

Continuous progressive action is denoted by "mo'gâng" = continuously; as—

Ma'râng thû mo-gâng'dai. Raining continually is.	It is continually raining.

Past Participle in "dai."

This participle is used in both a passive and active sense. Its use in a passive sense has already been illustrated at page 18 *ante*.

It is likewise used as a verbal noun, though as often as not the bare root of the verb does as well. When used as a verbal noun, it does not take the case-endings—

EXAMPLES.

Nâ'nâ kâ'dai n'ga'jâ"â,* Your writing bad	or, nâ'nâ kâ n'ga'jâ"â.*	Your writing is bad.
Nyê nâng ga-jâ'â.* My hearing good.		My hearing is good.

It is used in an active sense to denote the *agent* or *doer* of the action expressed by the verb; as—

EXAMPLES.

La-gû'dai Sing"pho bok'nî† Thieves (*lit.*, stealing) persons shin'yâng phrông'hâ dark while fled.	The thieves fled in the dark.
Ma-nau'dai jan bâ'dai. Dancers tired are.	The dancers are tired.

---

* Adjectival "â," *vide* foot-note, page 11 *ante*.

† This "nî" appears to be redundant, as "bok" alone is sufficient to denote plurality.

The agent may be made more emphatic by adding "wâ" to the participle, but the participial suffix "dai" is shortened to "da" for the sake of euphony; as—

La-gû'da"wâ * =thief (one who steals, stealing man).
Ma-nau'da"jan*=dancer, female.

Relation of Cause and Effect.

Cause is expressed by the word "ning'khân" to which the locative particle "î" is added. It means *because*; as—

Examples.

Sî'dai ning-khân'î ngai sâ'hâ. That account on I went.	On that account I went.
Mâng kâ-sî'dai ning-khan'î krap'dai. Child hungering because crying is	The child is crying, because it is hungry.
Nam ma-dî'dai ning khân'î n'khat'-â. Jungle wetting because not burn will.	The jungle will not burn; because it is wet.
N'dai ken'sûsû'dôn ding'lâ ngâ'dai ning-khân'î lasi'dai. This bullock old being because thin is.	This bullock is thin, because it is old.

Effect is expressed by using the demonstrative pronoun "sî'dai" with the participial suffix "dî" attached.

"Sî-dai'dî"=*that being*; that is, *for that reason*; as—

Examples.

Ngai mâng dûp'dî sî-dai'-dî krap'dai. I child beaten having on that account crying is.	I beat the child, therefore it is crying.
Lam ma-nen'dî sî-dai-dî ngai ka-tong'hâ. Road slippery being therefore I fell.	The road was slippery, therefore I fell.

* *Vide* page 5 *ante* for use of "wâ" and "jan."

The following illustrations will show the construction used in Singpho after verbs of *asking*, *entreating*, *commanding*, *seeing*, *hearing*, and *feeling*.

EXAMPLES.

Ngai kûm'phrông da-lâ'mâ khi'goi I silver rupee a he from phi'hâ. solicited.	I asked him for a rupee.
Khi shi'râ sâ * nâng-a'jo ngai'fê He with go accompany to me san'hâ. asked.	He asked me to accompany him.
Khi'fê ma-nau-â'jo san-i' ?† Her dance to ask ?	Shall I ask her to dance ?
Ngai sâ-a'jo â'khâng phi'hâ. I go to order solicited.	I begged him to let me go.
Khi ngai 'fê dûng ‡ ngû'hâ. He me sit bade.	He bade me sit down.
Khi'fê di'dai§ ngai mû'hâ *or* khi Him doing I saw *or* he di'yâng ngai mû'hâ. doing when I saw.	I saw him do it..
Khi mâng'fê dûp'yâng ngai He you striking when I mû'hâ. saw.	I saw him strike you.
Ngai khi'fê ngû'dai§ nâng'hâ. I him saying heard.	I heard him say it.
De-bru'goi si'nat gâp'dai§ ngai Debrughur at gun firing I nâng'hâ. heard.	I heard the Debrughur firing.
Mû tsi-gâ'dai§ nâng ngût kûn. Thundering hear able.	Can you hear the thunder?
Dûm-shûn'dai§ ngai dûm'hâ. Earthquaking I felt.	I felt the earthquake.
Nâ'nâ la-gôn'gi ma-shop'dai§ nâng Your leg on touching you dûm-há'khâ". felt.	Did you feel him touch your leg?

---

* "Nâng" means to accompany.
† Interrogative "i."
‡ "Dûng," this is the root of the verb used for the infinitive.
§ These are all verbal nouns.

12. Passive Voice.

There is no passive voice in Singpho.

Desire, in the sense of require, *physical necessity*, and *obligation*, are all expressed by the verb "râ," in its negative form "n'râ;" as—

Examples.

Ngai'fê yâm lô-î'mâ râ'dai. Me to powder little necessary is.	I want a little powder.
Ngai shî'râ gâ ma'tâng* râ-dai'î. I with coverse require.	Do (you) desire to speak to me?
Khrûng'dî ngâ a'jo shâ râ'dai	A man must eat to live.
Nâng sâ râ. You go must.	You must go.
Dêng'gâ ngai sâ râ. Then I go must.	Then I must go.
Nâng kû'lî yâ râ. You coolies give must.	You must give coolies.
Sing'pho yông yông sî râ'dai. Men all die must.	All men must die.

Moral necessity (*duty*, *right*, *wrong*) is expressed by the adjective "ai" = *good*, *right*, *proper* in its negative form "ng'ai" = wrong (opposite of right) or by the verb "âng" in its negative form "n'ang;" as—

Examples.

Ma'sû gâ tsî'gâ† ng'ai'dai. False word speak wrong is.	It is wrong to tell a lie.
Ngai sâ âng'dai. I go ought.	I ought to go.

Inclination, *wish*, &c., are expressed by the verbs "mit" and "mî'yû," in their negative forms "n'mit, n'mîyû," as—

Examples.

Shâ mî-yû'dai. Eat wish.	I wish to eat.
Ngai ngâ n'mit'dai. I remain not wish.	I do not wish to remain.
Ngai yûp n'mî'yû"â (*or* n'mî'yû"dai) I sleep not wish.	I am not inclined to sleep.
Nâng ma'nau mî-yû"dai'î? You dance wish?	Do you wish to dance?

* "Gâ ma'tâng" means to converse.
† "Gâ tsî'gâ" to utter words, speak.

13. Causative Verbs.

These are formed by *attaching* the verb "sî'nûn*" in the imperative mood, to other root verbs; as—

EXAMPLES.

Ma'nau ...... dance (root).	Ma'nau sî-nûn'û	...	cause to dance.
Lâ .... take or bring.	Lâ ———	...	bring.
Sâ .... go.	Sâ ———	...	go.
Dûp............ beat.	Dûp ———	...	beat.
Ma'rî .... buy.	Ma'rî ———	...	buy.

"Sî-nûn'û" appears to mean *to cause*, or *effect by agency.*

2. The conjugation of the verb "sî'nûn" is quite regular. The following illustrations show it with the tense suffixes attached; as—

EXAMPLES.

Ngai mû'khôn bok'fê nâng'goi ma'nau sî-nûnhâ. I young women here dance caused.	I made the girls dance here.
La-gû'da"wât† sing'pho ga'rim sî-nûn'gâ. Stealing man seize cause will.	I will have the thief seized.
Mâng'fê pot khûm sî-nûn'û. Child angry don't make.	Do not make the child angry.
Nam that'dai yâp sî-'nûn'û. Jungle thick is cut cause.	The jungle is thick, have it cut.
Mû-khon'nî"fê ma'nau si-nûn'yâng nî'fê lâ'hû jô-â'î ‡? Young women dance cause if them liquor give will.	If (I) make the young women dance, will (you) give them liquor?
La-gû'da"wât† ga'rim sî-nûn'dî ngai wâ'gâ. Thief seize caused having I quit will.	Having caused the thief to be seized, I will depart.

3. Transitive verbs are formed by prefixing "sî" or "tsî" to the root, some verbs therefore may be said to acquire a *causative form* when "sî" or "tsî" is prefixed to them; as—

EXAMPLES.

Krâ = dry (neuter).	Sî'krâ = to dry (active).
Khât = burn (do.).	Sî'khât = burn.
	Sî'gau = call (invite, or command to come or be present).

---

* Often pronounced "tsî'nûn." It means to empower, authorise, &c., as much as to cause.

† "La-gû'da"wa sing'pho" = The man *that* stole. The construction is participial, the "dai" (shortened to "da" for sake of euphony) being equivalent to the relative pronoun in English.

‡ Interrogative "î"

Sî'krit = frighten.
Sî'mât = lose.
Sî'lûn = boil (make hot).
&c. &c.,

EXAMPLES.

M'bá krâ'dai. Cloth dry is.	The cloth is dry.
M'bá sî-krâ'û. Cloth dry.	Dry the cloth.
Mâng phûng sî-krit'û. Child don't frighten.	Do not frighten the child.
Wan n'tâ khât'â. Fire house burn will.	The fire will burn the house.
N'tâ si-khât-û. House burn.	Burn the house.
N'chin lûm'ī* ? Water hot ?	Is the water hot.
N'chin sî-lûm'û Water heat	Heat the water.

14. COMPOUND VERBS.

Compound verbs are extensively used in Singpho. They are formed by (*a*) compounding one verbal root with another, (*b*) combining a noun with a verb; (*c*) combining a participle with a verb; (*d*) combining a noun or adjective with the auxiliary verb "ngâ" and the verb "tai" = *to become*, or "qui" = *about, on the point of*. When thus formed, the compound verb is conjugated as a simple one; as—

(*a*) **EXAMPLES.**

Sat ma'gau .... kill outright (*lit.* sat = kill, ma'gau= throw away).
Bai'wâ .... return } "Bai" is equivalent to the
Bai'yâ .... restore } English prefix "re."
Dî'ngût .... do able (dî‡ do, ngût-able).
Sâ'ngût .... go do (sâ=go).
Shâ'mi'yû................ eat inclined (shâ = eat).
Yûp'gok .... snore (yûp = sleep).
&c. &c.,

(*b*) **EXAMPLES.**

Ga'grî kâp .... dirty (ga'grî = dirt).
Ning'gûn dat .... use force (ning'gûn = force, &c).
Sai'krat .... bleed (sai=blood, krat = fall).
Ching'bô .... weed (ching = weed, bô = pull up).
Mî'grip .... wink (mî = eye.)
Mûng'lî dî .... work (mûng'li=work, dî=do.)

---

* Interrogative "ī."

Pa gâ gâ.................. trade (pa'gâ=trade, barter).
Gâ tsî'gâ..... .... talk (utter words).

(c) EXAMPLES.

Ga-lûn'dî sat .... pierce to death (ga'lûn=pierce, sat=kill).
Ga-rim'dî rêm .... seize (and) hold or keep (ga'rim=seize, rêm=keep).
Sâ'dî san .... go (and) ask (sâ=go, san=ask).
Dat'dî ngû............... send (and) tell (dat=send, ngû=tell).
Lâ'dî wâ.................. take (and) return (lâ=take, wâ = quit).
Tam'dî lû .... search (and) find (tâm=search, lû=obtain).
Thâ'dî lû .... find accidentally (thâ=pick up).
Noi'dî dau .... hang up (noi=hang up, dau=place, put).
&c., &c.

Ngâ'î* khî'fê ga-lûn'dî sat'hâ. Buffalo him piercing killed.	The buffalo horned him to death.
Ngai mû'yâng khrûng'dî ngâ'dai.† I seeing when living is.	When I saw (it), (it) was was alive.

(d) EXAMPLES.

Ning'gûn ngâ.............. possessing strength.
Ning'gûn tai .... becoming strong.
Ding'lâ tai .... ——— old.
Thû qui .... falling, about to.
Sî qui .... dying, do.
&c., &c.

2. As in Miri and Kachári, verbal tense suffixes may be put directly to nouns, adjectives, or adverbs; as—

EXAMPLES.

Ning'thoi = light (not dark).

Ning'thoi thoi'dai........... is light.
" hâ .... was light.
" â .... will be light.
" yâng .... if, when light.
" dî .... being light.

Ka'chî = cold.

Ka-chî 'dai .... is cold.
" hâ .... was cold.
" â .... will be cold.
&c., &c.

Mû'khûp = cloudy.

Mû-khûp'dai .... is cloudy.
" hâ .. .. was cloudy.
" â .... will be cloudy.
&c., &c.

---

* Nominatival "î," denoting agent.
† Present tense used to express past time, *vide* page 31 *ante*.

Ngût=able.

Ngût'dai .... is able.
„ hâ .... was able.
„ â .... will be able.
&c., &c.

Qui=about, on the point of.

Qui'dai—
&c., &c.

and numerous others.

A few sentences containing nouns, adjectives, and adverbs with verbal tense suffixes attached :—

Dai'nî ka-chî'dai. To-day cold is.	It is cold to-day.
Khî'â* mâng'â* prât'î phrâ-phrû'dai. His childhood pretty is.	He was a pretty child.
Ga-jâ'â , (*or* ga'jâ tai â). Good will be (good become will).	It will be (become) good.
Khî mî-pai'yâng mi n'mû'â. He blind being eyes not see will.	If he is blind, he can*not* see.
Nûm'shâ n'nâ-phâng'dai. Woman not deaf is.	The woman is not deaf.
M'bûng bûng'dî phûn ka'pâng tông'hâ. *Lit.* wind blown having tree uproot fell.	Being windy, the tree was uprooted and fell.
N'dai sat† ngâ'dî gâ-tsî'gâ ng'ai'dai. Such words utter wrong is.	It is wrong to utter such words.
Ram ram dî'dî man n'khong dî'û. Equal doing shares two do (*or* make).	Divide (it) equally into two shares.

3. Again (as in Miri and Kachári) the noun is occasionally repeated in the verb, expressing, as it were, the kindred action; as—

EXAMPLES.

Dûn'vê = broom.
Dûn'vê vê'dai = is sweeping.
hâ = was sweeping.
â = will sweep.
û = sweep (imperative).
yâng = sweeping, if, when do.
dî = having swept.

Pa'nêp = mat.
Pa'nêp nêp'dai = mat is spreading.
hâ = mat was spreading.
â = mat will spread.
&c., &c.

---

* "Â" used instead of "nâ," the full possessive sign, *vide* footnote on page 17 *ante*.

† "N'dai sat" = this like.

The same with—

Pan'râng=raised platform ("chang.")	Ning'thoi=light, not dark.
Dûm'shûn=earthquake.	La'lâm=fathom.
Ning'shin=night, dark.	La'khâm=span.
M'bûng=wind.	Bom'bâm=" pagri."
La'dông=cubit.	La'khon=bracelet.
Phûn'sî=fruit (*lit.*, tree seed).	Pa'gâ=trade.

and a few others.

15. Intensive Particles.

There are no intensive particles in Singpho.

16. Interrogative Form of Verbs.

The interrogative particles are "î" and "khâ." They appear to be interchangeable, though "khâ" is apparently more often used with the past indicative tense than "î." These particles are often tacked on to adjectives, adverbs, &c.

Examples.

Ma' râng thû-dai'î"? Raining is?	Is it raining?
N'dai khâ shûng-â'î? (*or* shûng ngâ'î"?) This river deep will be?	Is this water deep?
N'dai nî'nâ lai'î"? This your custom?	Is this your custom?
Khî'nî Sing-pho 'î"? They Singphos?	Are they Singphos?
Ma'gui gui-'lâ'î"? Elephant male?	Is (it) a male elephant?
Nâng kâ-sî'dai"î"? You hungry are?	Are you hungry?
Nâng sâ* mit-dai'î"? You go wish?	Do you wish to go?
N'dai î'nâ lî'î"? This our boat?	Is this our boat?
Ngai'fê tsî-'gâ'hâ"khâ"? Me call have?	Did (you) call me?
Mû† tsî-gâ'dai nâng-hâ'hkâ"? Thundering heard did?	Did (you) hear the thunder?
Sâ-heb'fê mû-hâ'khâ"? Saheb see did?	Have (you) seen the Saheb?
Ngai jû'î"? I burn?	Shall I burn it?
Ngai ning shin-gâ'î"? I sing shall?	Shall I sing?
Nâng ning'shin ngût-â'î"? You sing able will?	Can you sing?
Nâng Sing'pho gâ sû ngût-â'î"? You Singpho language speak able will?	Can you speak Singpho?

* Root of verb used for infinitive. † Mû tsî'gâ=*lit.*, heavens or sky call. "Mû tsî-gâ'dai" is a verbal noun, *vide* page 37 *ante*.

2. Negative interrogatives are formed by the suppressed sound of the letter "n" before the verb, and the interrogative particle "kha" or "î" tacked on to the root or tense suffix, as—

EXAMPLES.

Nang n'ma-chî-dai'î"? You not ill are?	Are you not ill?
Sing'dî n'rai'î"? True not is?	Is it not true?
Nâng n'mû-dai'î"? You not seeing?	Do you not see it?
Nî'nâ lî'sham n'ngâ dai'î"? Your paddles not possess?	Have you no paddles?
Nâng shî'rông n'mû-hâ'khâ"? You tiger not saw?	Have you not seen the tiger?
Nang n'sâ-â'î"? You not go will?	Will you not go?
Nâng phûng'yot n'ngût-â'î"? You swim not able will?	Can you not swim?

3. Interrogative *alternatives*, or alternatives *expressive of doubt* are formed by using the conjunction "kûn," = *or*.

This "kûn" may be termed the future interrogative auxiliary, although occasionally it is used with other tenses; as—

EXAMPLES.

Sî'dai lî phring'dî* ngâ kûn gû'man nga? That boat full or empty is?	Is that boat full or empty?
Nâng khî'fê dûp kûn n'dûp? You him beat or not beat?	Did you strike him or not?
Thin* ngâ kûn? Sink will?	Will it sink? (doubtful).
Nâ'nâ la'khon ngai'nâ la-tâ'î shâng kûn? Your bracelet my hand on go on will?	Will your bracelet go on my arm?

4. The interrogative particle "î" is sometimes tacked on to "kûn;" as—

EXAMPLES.

Ma'râng thû kûn† î? Rain fall?	Will it rain?
Khî nâng'goi dû‡ kûn† î? He here arrived?	Has he arrived here?

---

* These are compound verbs, *vide* page 42 *ante*.

† Here the speaker seeks a reply, being himself uncertain on the point.

‡ Bare root of verb used to denote past time, *vide* page 31 *ante*.

6. As a rule, the interrogative particles are *dispensed with* when any word (such as an interrogative pronoun, or an adverb) in the sentence *implies* interrogation; as—

EXAMPLES.

Da-mâ'ī* tsî-gâ'doi? Who calling?	Who is calling?
Nâng da-mâ'nan lû'hâ? You who from got?	From whom did you get (it)?
Nâng'fê ma-khai'mâ râ'dai? You what require?	What do you want?
Lî ga'dê ga-lû'dai? Boat how long is?	What is the length of the boat?
Ngai'na lî ga-dê-na'wâ? My boat which?	Which is my boat?
Nâng khî'fê ga-loi'mê mû'dai? You him when seeing?	When did you see him?
Ma'khai rai'dai? What being?	What is the matter?
Nâng wû ga'dê ma-rî'hâ? You fowls how many bought?	How many fowls did you purchase?

17. NEGATIVE FORM OF VERBS.

As with substantive so with root verbs *negation* is expressed by the *suppressed sound* of the letter "n" put *before* the verb; as—

EXAMPLES.

Khî n'gâ n'thai'dai. He earth not ploughing.	He is not ploughing.
N'dai la'khon n'shâng'dai. This bracelet not go on.	This bracelet won't go on.
Ngai n'sâ'â I not go will.	I will not go.
Ngai nâ'nâ gâ n'nâng'dai.† I your words not hearing.	I did not hear you.
Ngai phûng'yot n'ngût'â. I swim not able.	I cannot swim.
N'ka-chî'yâng ngai pa'lông n'phûng'â. Not cold being I coat not wear will.	Not being cold, I will not wear a coat.
Khî'fê n'mû'dai‡ ning-khân'ī bai-wâ'hâ Him not seeing because returned.	Not having seen him, I returned.

---

* Nominatival "ī."
† Present tense used to denote past time, *vide* page 31 *ante*.
‡ Verbal noun.

2. The negative particle may be attached directly to adjectives; as—

EXAMPLES.

Ngai n'ma-chî'â*. I not ill.	} I (am) not ill.
Khî n'le-bê'â*. He not lame.	} He (is) not lame.
Lam'î† n'ma-nên'â*. Road not slippery.	} The road (is) not slippery.
N'nî'â*. Not near.	} Not near.
N'lo'â* Not sufficient.	} Not sufficient.

N.B.—In lieu of the adjectival "â," the auxiliary "dai" might be used with all the above examples; as—

Ngai n'ma-chî'dai I not ill am.	} I am not ill.
&c.,	&c.

3. The prohibitive negative has already been noticed at page 34 *ante*.

18. ADVERBS.

These may be classified as follows—

OF TIME.

Dai'nî.......... to-day.	Sing-oi'î§............... before.
M'phô'nî .... to-morrow.	Ning-dim'î§........... after.
Phrâ‡'nê ... day after that.	Dai'ning .... this year.
Mâ'nê........... yesterday.	Dê'ning .... next year.
Mâ'nî .... day before ditto.	Ma'ning .... last year.
Mâng'nî .... Ditto.	Ga-loi'mang............ again.
Lî-nî'mê......... daily.	Yâ'dû, galai............ yet (up to present time).
Têng'krê ...... all day.	Made by using "ga-loi'mang" with a negative verb, *vide* examples given *post*. } never.
Ma-nâp'î§ ...... dawn, early morning.	Ga-noi'hê *or* gui ... nearly, almost
Yâ .... now.	Chi-nâ'nong .... always.
Ning shin'î§ ... at night.	Lo'hâ .... ago, past.
Yâ ga-lâng'mâ.. once more.	Made by participle "yâng." } whilst.
Ga-loi'nau phrat. since when.	
Yat .... soon, presently.	
Ga'loi ga-loi'mê. sometimes.	

* *Vide* foot-note, page 11 *ante*. The use of this "â" has puzzled me a good deal.

† Nominatival "î."

‡ "Prâ'nî" *or* "Phâng'nî."

§ "Î" and "goi" locative case postpositions.

Of Place.

Nâng'goi* ...... here.
Dai'goi* ...... there (near and in sight).
Ôrâ'goi*......... there (some distance off).
Thô'goi*......... there (far away, or out of sight).
Sing-oi'î* *or* man'î* in front.
Rau .... together.
Khâ'khû .... up stream.

Nî'goi* .... near.
Shî'râ yông'goi* ... everywhere (*lit.*, all places in).
Dai-goi*'nan......... thence.
Sing-gan'î* .... outside.
Ta-qui'î* .... inside.
Khâ'nam .... down stream.
Ning-shâng'î* ...... above.
Ka-tai'î* *or* m'pû'î* below.

Of Quality.

Song song......... wholly, entirely.
N'dai sot .... thus, in this manner.
Ai rai'dî .... carefully.
N'aidî .... badly.
Ai'dî................ well.
Chû .... alone.

Kûn .... probably, perhaps.
Sing'dî .... certainly.
Ning-khân'î* ... therefore.
Ga'lau ga'lau ... quickly.
Dai'dî .... therefore.
Sot................... like (in a like manner).
Dêng'gâ .... then.

Of Quantity.

Jat .... more.
Shî'bâ *or* jam'ram much (in a great degree).
Made by interrogative pronoun "ga-dê'mâ" and participle in "dî" with "mang" added. } as much as, as many.
Dai'thêng .... this much.
Sî'dai thêng ...... that.

M'phû .... about, approximately.
No word, made by numeral "ai"= one, repeated, or by using "kau" =part, with numeral suffix "mâ." } some.
Chû... .... only.
Mang .... also.

Interrogative.

Ma-khai'dî=why?
Ga-dê'goi *or* dê'goi=where?
Ga-loi'mê=when?

Ga-dê'goi" nan=whence?
Gi-ning'dî=how (in what manner)?

Ga-dê'mâ=how many, much, often, &c.

---

* "î" and "goi" locative case postpositions.

2. Adverbs are placed *before* verbs and adjectives; sometimes they begin a sentence.

EXAMPLES.

Illustrating how Adverbs are used.

Dai'nî ka-thet'â. To-day warm.	*To-day* it is warm.
Ma'nî ka-chî'â. Yesterday cold.	*Yesterday* (it was) cold.
Khî m'phô'nî Sadiya goi'nan sâ'â. He to-morrow Sadiya from go will.	He will leave Sadiya *to-morrow.*
Mâ'nî ngai shan ai'mâ gâp'hâ. Day before yesterday I deer one shot.	*The day before yesterday* I shot a deer.
Ngai li-nî'mê khâ-shin'dai. I daily bathe.	I bathe *daily*.
Sî'dai sî-tâ'î li-nî'mê ma'râng thû'dai. Died moon in daily rain falling.	It rained *daily* last month.
Sî-dai si-nî'nâ m'prat n'mû'hâ That days since not seen	I have not seen (him) since *that day.*
Dai-ning'î mâng'wâ pâ'dai.* This year in child born.	The child was born *this year.*
Dê-ning'î ngai Hûkong'goi sâ'gâ. Next year in I Hukong to go will.	I shall visit Hukong *next year.*
Ma-ning'î mâm n'ga-já'â. Last year in paddy not good.	*Last year's* dhan (crop) (was) bad.
Ma-nâp'î nûm-shâ'î † mâm thû'dai. Dawn at women paddy husk.	In the *early morning* the women pound out rice.
Yâ'gâ nâ'dai. Now tabooing.	(The village) is *now* tabooing.
Yâ ngai'fê yâ'î. ‡ Now me give.	Give (it) to me *now.*
Sî-nâ'î sâ krit'dai. Night in go afraid am.	I am afraid to go *at night.*
Yâ'mang ga-lâng'mâ dî'û. *Lit.*, now also once do.	Do it once again.
Nâng ga-loi'nan ma-chî'dî ngâ'dai. § You when from ailed have.	*Since when* have you been ill?

---

* Present tense used to denote past time, *vide* page 31 *ante*.

† Nominatival "î."

‡ Imperative suffix.

§ This is a compound verb, *vide* page 42 *ante*.

Ga'lâng ga'lâng ngai'fê Sometimes (*lit.*, once, once) me ngan'dai. scolds.	(He) scolds me *sometimes.*
Ga'lâng ga'lâng ngai lâ'hû lû'dai. Sometimes I liquor drink.	*Sometimes* I drink liquor.
Ngai ga'loi ga'loi* mang shan I whenever deer mû-yang'gâ gap'dai. seeing shall shoot.	*Whenever* I see a deer I shoot (it).
Mâng'wâ ga'loi ga'loi mang ngan yâng Child whenever scolding gâ krâp'dai. shall cries.	*Whenever* I scold the child (it) cries.
Khî dû'dai sing-oi'î ngai sâ'gâ. He arriving before I go shall.	I will go *before* he arrives.
Ma'râng thû'dai sing-oi'î sâ'û. Rain falling before go.	Go *before* the rain falls.
Ngai sâ'dai ning-dim'î nâng ma'khai I going subsequently you what di'dai. do.	What did you do *after* my departure?
Nâng mû'dai† ning-dim'î ngai shan You seeing subsequently I deer n'khong gâp'hâ. two shot.	I shot two deer *after* I saw you.
Ga-lai'mang dî'û. Again do.	Do it *again.*
Khî yâ'dû mang n'prûhâ. He yet even not come has.	He has not *yet* come.
Yâ'dû mang jân n'shânghâ. Yet even sun not set has.	It is not *yet* sunset.
Khî yâ dû mang n'lû'â. He yet even not drank has.	He has not *yet* drunk.
Khî yâ dû n'wâ'hâ"dai. He yet not gone has.	He has not gone *yet.*
Ngai ga-lai'mang n'ngû'hâ. I never not said.	I never said (so).
Ngai ga-lai'mang n'sâ'â. I never not go will.	I will *never* go.
Shan ga-noi'hê sî'dai. Deer almost dead is.	The deer is *almost* dead.
Or shan sî-qui'dai. Deer dying about is.	The deer is *about* dying.

* "Ga'lai ga'loi mang" means, *lit.*, when, when, even.
† "Mû'dai" is a verbal noun.

N'khong ning lô'hâ ngai Ka-lî-ka-tâ'- Two years ago I Calcutta goi" ngâng'dai. in was.	Two years *ago* I was in Calcutta.
Khrû yâ lô'hâ sî'dai sing'pho nang'goi Six days ago that man here ngâ'dai.* is.	Six days *ago* that man was here.
Nyê † ma-son'î prû'û. My near to come.	Come *near* me.
Khâ ma-son'î dau'û. River near to place.	Put (it) *near* the river.
Shî'râ yông goi dû'bông mû'dai. Places all in goitre see.	(I) see goitre *everywhere*.
N'ta sing-gan'î ka-chî'dai ta-qui'î House outside cold is inside ka-thet'dai. warm is.	*Outside* the house (it) is cold, *inside* (it) is warm.
Sing-oi'î sâ'û. Front in go.	Go in *front*.
Sâ-hâ'pâ mon'î châp'û. Saheb front of stand.	Stand in *front* of the Saheb.
Sing'pho n'dai yon rau mûng'lî Men these two together work rai'dai.* doing.	These two men were working *together*.
Lî rau tsî-jûp'dî dá'û. Boats together tie.	Tie the (two) boats *together*.
N'dai khâ jam'ram shûng'â. This river very deep.	This river (is) *very* deep.
Gên jam'ram ka-chî'dai. Snow very cold is.	Snow is *very* cold.
M'ba n'dai tsi'bâ jê'â. Cloth this much torn.	This cloth is *much* torn.
Ngai nâng'goi li-ning'mâ m'phû I here year a about ngâ'gâ. remain shall.	I shall remain here *about* a year.
N'dai ma-rêng'î sing'pho ma-sûm'tsâ This village in persons three hundred m'phû ngâ'dai. about are.	There are *about* 300 people in this village
Ken'sû ai ai‡ sau'dai ai ai laî'dai. Cows some fat are some lean are.	*Some* cows are fat, *some* thin.
Phûn kau kau gâ‡ wâ'dai kau kau gâ Woods some float some thin'dai. sink.	*Some* woods float, *some* sink.

---

* Present tense used to denote past time.

† This is the same as Assamese "môr ûsôrôtê."

‡ "Ai ai" means, *lit.*, one, one, and "kau kau gâ" a part.

Wû ga-dê'mâ mû-dî' mang ma-rî'û. Fowls as many seeing even buy.	Buy *as many* fowls *as* you see.
N'gû ga-dê'mâ lû ngût'dî mang lâû. Rice as much get able being even bring.	Bring *as much* rice *as* you can get.
Ngai wâ mang mûhâ. I pigs also saw.	I saw pigs *also*.
Nâng mang sâ-â'î″ ? You also go will ?	Will you *also* go ?
Ngai'nâ mâng prât li-ning'mâ chû rê. My child age year one only verily.	My child is *only* one year old.
Ngai'nâ mâng ai'ma chû rê. My child one only verily.	I have *only* one child.
Ga-dê'mâ chân'dî mang. How much far being even.	*However* far it may be.
Sî'dai mâng mâ'â song-song'î″* ? That child dumb entirely ?	Is that child *quite* dumb ?
Shan sî song song rai'dai. Deer dead quite is.	The deer is *quite* dead.
Ai rai'dî† sâ'û lam jam'ram ma-nen'dai. Carefully go road very slippery is.	Go *carefully*, the road is very slippery.
Ngai chû sâ n'ngût'â. I alone go not able.	I cannot go *alone*.
Mâng'fê chû khûm tsî-kram'û. Child alone don't	Don't leave the child *alone*.
Khâ tûng kau'â. River rise probably will.	The river will *probably* rise.
Ngai m'pho'nî sing'dî sâ'gâ‡. I morrow truly go shall.	I will *certainly* go to-morrow.
Ga'lau ga'lau sâ'û. Quickly go.	Go *quickly*.
Khî si'qui″dai *or* khî lo-î-mâ'goi″- He die about is he little (time) in sî'â. die will.	He is *about* to die.
N'dai sot dî'û. This wise do.	Do it *like this*.
Khî kai'pet sot rai'dî phûng-yot'dai. He duck resembling swims.	He swims *like* a duck.
Khî chau'phâ sot rai'dî gâ tsî-gâ'daî. He king resembling talks.	He talks *like* (as if he were) a king.
Nâng ngai'fê ma-khai'dî chî-ga'dai§ ? You me why calling ?	*Why* did you call me ?

---

* Interrogative particle tacked on to an adverb, *vide* page 45 *ante*.

† "Ai" = well, properly "rai'dî" participle past of substantive verb "rai," so that "ai rai dî" freely translated, means carefully.

‡ Here again we have the future tense suffix "gâ" used to denote distant future time, *vide* foot-note page 32 *ante*.

§ Present tense used to denote past time, *vide* page 31 *ante*.

Nâng khî'fê ga-dê'goi mû'hâ ? You him where seen ?	*Where* did you see him ?
Khî'nî ga-loi'mê dî'hâ ? They when did ?	*When* did they do it ?
Khî gadê'goi dî'kûn″* ngai sû n'ngût'â. He where do I say unable.	I don't know where he did (it).
Khî gi'ning dî-hâ-dai'kun″* He how (in what manner) done has ngai n'choi'â. I not known.	I don't know *how* he did (it).
Nâng ga dê'goi dî† ? You where do ?	*Where* will you do it ?
Khî ga-dê'goi dî-dai'kûn* ngai d'choi'â. He where doing I not know.	I don't know *where* he did (it).
Nâng ga dê'goi″nau sâ'dai ? You whence coming ?	*Whence* do you come ?

3. The participial suffix "dî" seems to be used as an adverbial particle answering to the English "ly;" as—

Ai'dî = well, properly.	N'ai'dî = badly.
Sing'dî = certainly.	Têng'dî = truly.

Ram-ram'dî = equally.

Lî ai'dî git'û. Boat well tie.	Tie the boat well (properly).

4. A few of the adjectives and adverbs are repeated, apparently for the sake of *emphasis*; as—

Ga'lau ga'lau = quickly.
Chau'sû chau'sû = slowly.
Ram'ram = equal, adequate.
Song song = entirely.
Nong nong = always.
Jam'ram = very.
Yong yong = all.
&c., &c.

Prepositions.

(*In Singpho terminals or postpositions.*)

Ma-son'goi‡ Nî'goi‡	= adjacent to.	Nan‡ = from. I‡ *or* goi‡ = in, at, by, &c.

---

* "Kûn" used as an interrogative particle expressive of doubt.

† "Dî" is the root of the verb used to denote the future tense, *vide* page 31 *ante*.

‡ Locative case postpositions.

Ta-gui'î*	Within inside.
Sing-gan'î*	Without, outside.
Ka-tâ'î* *or* †n'ngâ yang.	Not with, destitute of, &c.
Da'pham, *or* tsî râ.	With.
M'pû'î*	down, beneath.
Khâ-âng'î*	In the middle.
La-pân'î*	Among, between
A'jo	For.
Sing-oi'î*	Before.
Ning-tsâng'î*	Upon, at the top of, &c.

EXAMPLES.

(*Illustrating how used.*)

Nyê ma-son'goi sâ'û. My side to move.	Some *near* (to) me.
Wan nî-da‡'goi dau'û. Fire near to place.	Put (it) *near* (to) the fire.
Yû ning'krû ka-tâ'î ngâ'dai. Mouse hole inside is.	The mouse is *inside* the hole.
Sing-gau'î ka-thet'dai. Outside warm is.	It is warm *outside*.
Ma'gui ning-tsâng'î jau'û. Elephant upon mount. Ma-gui'goi jau'û. Elephant on mount.	Get *upon* the elephant.
N'tâ ning-tsâng'î wû ai'mâ ngâ'dai. House on top of bird one is.	There is a bird *on the top of* the house.
Rî tsî'râ tsî-jûp'û. Cane with tie (fasten).	Tie it *with* cane.
Lî khâ-âng'î dûng'û. Boat middle of sit.	Sit in the *middle* of the boat.
Wan you ngai la-pân'î khûm châp'û. Fire both I between don't stand.	Do not stand *between* me and the fire.
Khâ bûm n'khong la-pân'î yông'dai. River mountains two between. flows.	The river flows *between* the two mountains.
Ning'rî n'ngâ'yâng khî sâ§ n'ngût'â. Spear not possessing if he go unable. *or*	He cannot go *without* a spear.
Ning'rî ka'tâ§ sâ§ n'ngût'â. Spear without go unable.	*Without* a spear cannot go.

* Î=locative case postposition.

† "N'ngâ yâng"=substantive verb "ngâ," in its negative form, with participal suffix "yâng" added.

§ Mere root of verb used to denote the infinitive mood, *vide* page 34 *ante*.

Conjunctions.

Mang = and, also too, even.	Kûn = or, either.
Made by demonstrative pronoun "si'dai" = *that*, with participle in "dî" tacked on to it. } therefore.	Made by participle = whether.
	Made by participle in "dî" with "mang" = although.
Made by participle in "yâng." } if, when, &c.	N'lo = than.

Examples.

(Illustrating how used.)

Nâng mang ngai mang khî mang sâ'â.
You and I and he and go will.
} You and I and he will go.

This conjunction "mang" connects *words* only. In sentences where in English the conjunction *and* would be used, Singphos use a participle, as—

Examples.

Ching bok* bô'dî mo-gau'û.
Weeds uprooting throw away.
} Pull up the weeds, and throw them away.

Khî nyê n'tâ'î (*or* n'tâ ta-gui'î) shâng'dî nyê si'nat la-gû'dai.†
He my house in inside entering my gun stealing.
} He went into my house and stole my gun.

When put *after* a noun or pronoun, "mang" means *also*, *likewise*; as—

Examples.

Dai'goi ngai mang ngâ'dai.
There I also am.
} I also was there (*i.e.*, besides others).

Ngai shan mang gâp'hâ.
I deer also shot.
} I shot a deer also.

Ngai mang shan gâp'hâ.
I also deer shot.
} I also shot a deer.

The English conjunctions *neither*, *nor*, are likewise made by using "mang;" as—

Examples.

Lûm mang n'lûm ka'chî‡ mang n'kachî.‡
Warm and not warm cold and not cold.
} It is *neither* hot *nor* cold.

---

* "Ching"=weed, "bok" particle denoting plurality, *vide* page 7 *ante*.

† This is the present tense of the verb used to denote past time, *vide* page 31 *ante*.

‡ These are the mere roots of the verb, *vide* page 31 *ante*.

Khî ding'lâ mang n're sha'brâng He old (man) and not young man mang n'rê. and not.	He is *neither* old *nor* young.

EXAMPLES.

Illustrating how sentences containing "until" are construed.

Khî n'dû* ting'sâng ngâ'û. He not arrived until remain.	Remain *until* he comes.
Ma'râng n'phrong ting'sâng Rain not stop *lit.* runaway until ngai kring'gâ. I stay shall.	I shall remain *until* the rain stops.

Sometimes "la-pâ'n'î" = *between*, but which can, apparently, likewise be used to express *in the interval* (of time), is used instead of "ting'sâ;" as—

EXAMPLE.

Ngai sing'rî n'lâ† la-pân'î I rope not bringing interval in ken-sû'fê ga-rim'dî‡rêm'û. cow hold.	Hold the cow *until* I bring a rope.

EXAMPLES.

(with *either* ... *or.*)

Nâng kûn khî la-gû'dai. You or he lying are	*Either* you *or* he are lying.

This sentence might also be construed by using a participle; as—

Nang n'ma-sû-yâng'gâ" khî ma-sû'â.§ You not false being he false.	*Either* you *or* he are lying.

In sentences where in English the conjuction *either* is *alone* used (its correlative *or* being understood) "kûn" is not used in Singpho; as—

EXAMPLES.

Ga-dê-na'wâ" rai'dî mang ai'mâ *Lit.*, which being even one lagâ. take will.	I will take *either* (one or the other, understood).

---

* These are the mere roots of the verb, *vide* page 31 *ante.*

† "N'lâ" = root of lâ = *take*, in its negative form, that is suppressed sound of "n" prefixed to it. "N'lâ" is used in lieu of "n'lâ'dî" the participle.

‡ Compound verb first "ga'rim" = seize, with past participle "dî" suffixed and "rêm" = keep, with Imperative suffix proper "û."

§ Adjectival "â."

"Kûn" is used (as in English) with *numerals*; as—

EXAMPLE.

Ma'gui ga'dê ngâ'dai? ma'lî Elephants how many are? four kûn ma'ngâ ngâ'dai. or five are.	How many elephants are there? There are four *or* five.

EXAMPLES with *although* ... *yet*.

Khî'fê sû'dî mang ngai'fê Him saying even me n'yum'hâ. not believe did.	*Although* I told him, *yet* he would not believe me.
Ma'râng thû'dî mang lam kûm'pâ Raining even road muddy n'tai'dai (*or* kûm'pâ n'rê). not become is.	*Though* it rained, *yet* the road is not slippery.
Khî phûn châ* grau-da-goi'nan" He tree high exceedingly from krat'dai dai'dimang falling *lit*, being even (even so) n'sî'â. not die will.	*Though* he fell from off a very high tree, *yet* he was not killed.

As far as (*as much as*, *as many*, &c.) is made as follows—

EXAMPLES.

Ngai ga'dê m'phû sâ-da'kûn" I as far as going sî'dai dû khâ tâng'dai. that far river deep is.	The river was deep *as far as* I went.

PART III.—SYNTAX.

There is little to be said under this head with my present limited knowledge of the language.

The examples and explanatory remarks of the preceding pages have already given some insight into the structure of Singpho sentences, and, in order, if possible, further to elucidate the subject, I purpose now giving some additional typical and illustrative sentences arranged in groups, following the order of the different parts of speech, and numbered with reference to the sections bearing the same numbers in the Accidence.

1. The order of words in a predicative sentence are (1) subject, (2) direct object, (3) indirect object, (4) verb. *Occasionally* the direct *follows* the indirect object.

---

* "Châ grau'da" is a verbal adjective. The "da" is the participial suffix "dai" shortened to "da" for sake of euphony. "Phûn châ da goi nau" means from off a tree *which* is tall.

2. In an interrogative sentence the order is (1) subject, (2) indirect object, (3) direct object, (4) verb. *Occasionally* the direct object *precedes* the indirect one.

3. The adjective *generally* follows, though it *sometimes precedes* the noun it qualifies ("Sing'pho ga'jâ"=man bad, "nûm'shâ mî'yâm"= female slave.)

4. Relative clauses, and all constructions taking their place stand before antecedent clauses.

5. Interrogative pronouns stand *first* less often than in English.

6. Adverbs are placed *before* adjectives and verbs, and they occasionally *commence* a sentence.

In ordinary conversation Singbhos are very fond of tacking the particle "nâ" or "lô" on to the end of every sentence.

The first ("nâ") is apparently a sort of *persuasive* particle (equivalent to the Assamese "dê," as "jâ'bî dê"= go, won't you, or mind you, go), though often a mere expletive, and the second is apparently an emphatic, pure and simple.

EXAMPLES.

Nâng lâ'û nâ. You take.	You take (do or won't you).
Ngai sâ'gâ nâ. I go shall.	I shall go.
Khî dûp'da lô. He striking.	He is striking.

I.—NOUNS.

1. Gender.

Ngai'fê wû'râng n'khong wuvî mâ'ngâ râ'dai. Me cocks two hens five necessary.	I want two cocks (and) five hens.
Nyê'nâ ken'sû sû'dôn* ma'lî ngâ'dai. My bullocks four are.	I have four bullocks.
Ken'sû n'dai nâ'thûm rai'dai. Cow this barren is.	This cow is barren.
Khî'nâ sî'vî mâng n'khong lâ'sha mâng ai'mâ chû ngâ'dai. His female children two male children one only is.	He has two girls (children) and only one boy.

* "Dôn" is the root of a verb meaning to impair animals' testicles by pounding them.

N'gâ * gui n'dai gui-lâ'î" † ? Jackal this male ?	Is this a male jackal?
Ngai khai'khê ngâ'lâ ai'mâ gâp'dai.‡ I wild buffalo male one shot.	I shot a wild bull buffalo.
Ngâ'pho n'dai ngâ vî. Mithan this female.	This is a cow mithan.
Ngai'fê woi woi'lâ ai'mâ râ'dai. Me to monkey male one necessary.	I want a male monkey.
Wâ vi gâ§ li'ning goi n'khong'lâng yû'dai. Sows year in twice breed.	Sows breed twice a year.
Gûm'rang ‖ ngâ vî sidai la'gông le-bê'dai. Mare that leg lame is.	That mare is lame.
Khî'nâ lâ'shâ mî'yam ma'lî His male slaves four Nûmshâ mî'yam ma'sûm ngâ'dai. Female slaves three are.	He has four male and three female slaves.
Gûm'gai mî-pai'î"? Old woman blind?	Is the old woman blind?

2.—*Number.*

Pa'lâ u'dai bok ma-gô'dai. Arrows these bent are.	These arrows are bent.
N'dai sî-pâ'hî da-pham'î sâ sû.** These sipahis with go.	Accompany these sepoys.
N'dai'nî sing-pho'î"?†† These Singphos ?	Are these (people) Singphos ?
Mû'khon bok ma-nau-â'kha" ?†† Young women dance will ?	Will the young women dance ?
Kai'pet nî (*or* bok) khâ'î dat'û. Ducks water in let loose.	Put the ducks into the water.

---

* "N'gâ" = earth, "gui" = dog, so that "n'gâ gui" means, *lit.*, earth dog.

† Interrogative "î".

‡ Present tense used to denote past time, *vide* page 31 *ante*.

§ "Gâ" here is merely emphatic.

‖ This is apparently an irregular method of forming the feminine, *vide* page 6 *ante*.

** Imperative proper of root verb "sâ" go, *vide* foot-note page 34 *ante*.

†† "Î" and "khâ" interrogative particles.

Wû'dî bok ga-jâ-â'khâ"*? Eggs good?	Are the eggs fresh?

3.—Case.

Chû khrî'dai. Milk sour is.	The milk is sour.
Jân jâ'dai. Sun strong is.	The sun is hot.
Ngê pa'lông jê'dai. My coat torn is.	My coat is torn.
Ngâ'î † khî'fê ga'lûn‡ sat'dai. Buffalo him horning killed.	The buffalo horned him to death.
Ken'sû sû vî'nâ lâ'gông dô'hâ. Cow female leg broken.	The cow's leg is broken.
N'dai da'mâ § ning'rî? This whose spear?	Whose spear is this?
Wû pî-yen'hâ. Bird flown.	The bird has flown.
N'dai nâ§ gui châng'nâ‖ ka-shâ'î"¶? This your dog black' pup¶	Is this your black dog's pup?
Mâng'fê khûm tsî-krit'û. Child don't frighten.	Do not frighten the child.
Ngai'fê n'gû la'pai n'khong jo'û. Me rice handful two give.	Give me two handfuls of rice.
Lâ'shâ mâng** bok'fê lik'kâ†† mang Boys, male write and phat‖ mang tsî-rin'û. read and teach.	Teach the boys (to) read and write.
La'pû khû'î ngâ'dai. Snake hole in is.	The snake is in the hole.
Nâ'nâ mûng'goi ma-khai'mâ ngâ dai? Your basket in what is?	What is in your basket?
Nyê mûng'goi ma-khai'mâ‡‡ n'ngâ. My basket in what not is.	I have nothing in my basket.
Jan'î dâ'û. Sun in put.	Put it in the sun.
Bûm ning-tsâng'goi gên ngâ'dai. Hill top on snow is.	There is snow on top of the hill.

* "Khâ" interrogative particle.

† Nominatival "î" denoting agent.

‡ "Galûn" means to pierce with any sharp instrument. Here the root of the verb is used instead of the p.p. "Sat'dai" is the present tense used to denote past time, *vide* page 31 *ante*.

§ "Da'mâ" should be "da-mâ'nâ" and "nâ nâ'nâ," but possessive case suffix is occasionally omitted, *vide* page 16 *ante*.

‖ Here we have possessive case suffix tacked on to an adjective.

¶ Interrogative "î."

** "Bok"=particle of plurality with accusative case suffix.

†† Bare root of verbs "write," "read," used for infinitive, *vide* page 34 *ante*.

‡‡ "Ma-khai'mâ" something, "n'ngâ"=exists not.

Ngai khâ'î ma-gau'î"*? I river in throw?	Shall I throw it into the river?
Mâng-goi'nan ning'shî lâ'û. Child from knife take.	Take the knife from the child.
Nâng da-mâ-goi'nan lû'hâ? You who from got?	From whom did you get it?

4.—ADJECTIVES.

Ma'gui ga'bâ. Elephant large.	A large elephant.
Mû'khon n'khong. Young woman two.	Two young girls.
Ngâ'shan cha'phû. Fish rotten.	A rotten fish.
Châ'dai† phûn. High tree.	A high tree.
Lîsam n'dai mo-gô'dai Paddle this crooked is.	This paddle is crooked.
Phûn n'dai ga-jâ'î"‡? Tree *or* wood this good?	Is this wood good?
Shan cha'phû ngai shâ n'ngût'â. Meat rotten I eat unable.	I cannot eat high meat.

Comparison.

Lî n'dai ô'râ lîgoi nau ga'jâ. Boat this that boat from good.	This is a better boat.
Sî'dai n'lo'ê§ m'bâ ga'jâ yâ'û. That than cloth larger give.	Give me a larger cloth.
Sî'dai n'lo'ê§ n'chin ka'chî râ'dai. That than water cold want.	I want cooler water.
Si'lui n'prik n'lo kûm'chai si'lui dui Limes than oranges sweet grau' dai. very are.	Oranges are sweeter than limes.
N'dai wû n'lo ga'lâ‖ wû ga'bâ These fowls than Bengal fowls large grau' dai. very are.	English fowls are larger than these.

---

* "Ma'gau" is the mere root of the verb, but used here for the future tense, *vide* page 31 *ante*; the "î" tacked on is the interrogative particle.

† "Châ'dai phun," this is a participial construction, the "dai" being used to connect the noun "phun," and is equivalent to our relative pronoun.

‡ Interrogative "î."

§ This "ê" is merely euphonic.

‖ "Ga'lâ" means Bengal. Singphos, in common with all the other tribes on this frontier, speak of Bengal as if it was the *only* other country after Assam.

Nâ'nâ nûm'shâ mâng n'lo n'dai Your female child than this nûm'shâ mâng chå grau'i" ?* female child tall very?	Is this girl taller than your daughter.
Yong'â n'lo n'gû ga'jâ grau râ'dai. All than rice good very require.	I want the best rice.
Rûng n'dai yong'â n'lo ga'bâ grau Horn this all than large very dai. is.	This is the largest horn.
Yong'â n'lo n'thû ga'jâ grau'dai All than daos good very ga-dê'goi" nan lû'dai? where from procure?	Where do the best *daos* come from?

5.—Numeral Adjectives.

N'tâ khrû wan'i† khât'hâ. Houses six fire by burnt.	Six houses were burnt.
Gui ma'sûm rau khat'dai‡. Dogs three together fighting.	Three dogs were fighting together.
Chap sí'dai yon§ mû-ha' khâ"?‖ Bears those two seen have?	Did you see those two bears?
Ngai'fê kû'wâ khûn lâyâ'û§. Me bamboos twenty bring.	Bring me twenty bamboos.
Ngai shan ma'chat wâ ma'ngâ gâp'hâ. I deer eight pigs five shot.	I shot eight deer and five pig.
Da'lâ¶ n'khong'i** wû tsî. Rupees two with fowls ten. ma'ri n'gut-â'i" ?†† buy able will?	Can you buy ten fowls for two rupees?

Pronouns.

6.—Personal Pronouns.

Ngai kâsî'dai. I hungry am.	I am hungry.
Ngai khi'fê mûdai‡‡. I him seeing.	I saw him.

* This is the nominatival "i."

† Instrumental case postposition.

‡ Present tense used to denote past time, *vide* page 31 *ante*.

§ "Lâ yâ'û" is a compound verb. The first "lâ" is the root, and means *take*, and the second "yâ," with imperative suffix proper attached, means *give*.

‖ "Khâ" is one of the interrogative particles.

¶ "Da'lâ" is a numeral auxiliary denoting rupees, thus "kâm'phong da'lâ n'khong"=silver two rupees.

** Nominatival "i" denoting agent.

†† Interrogative "i."

‡‡ "Mû'dai" present tense of root verb "mû" used to denote past time, *vide* page 31 *ante*.

Nâng chû sâ'û. You alone go.	You go alone.
Khî dûm-shûn'dai* dûm'hâ. He earthquaking felt.	He felt the earthquake.
Khî lî khûp'hâ. He boat upset.	He upset the boat.
Nâng cha'rû lû î?† You mod drink?	Do you drink mod?
Î sing'pho rai'dai. We Singphos are.	We are Singphos.
(Si'nang or) Ì phen khat-î'?† We we fight?	Shall we fight?
Khî'nî nga qui'dai. They fishing.	They are fishing.
Khî-nî'fê mo-dûn'û. Them to show.	Show it to them.
Khî-nî'nâ ning'ri ga-lû'dai. Their spears long are.	Their spears are long.
Î yông mû'dai.‡ We all saw.	We all saw it.
Î phen khat n'mî-yû'â". We fight undesirous.	We don't want to fight.

7.—Relative Pronouns.

Se'nat gâp-da'wa thô ra'wâ. Gun firer that man.	He is the man that fired the gun.
Ma-sû'dai§ nûm'shâ. Lying woman.	The woman that told a lie (lie spoken woman).
Tsi'rông mû'dai§ sing'pho ngai'fê Tiger seen man me mo-dûn'û. show.	Show me the man who saw the tiger.
Ngai non'dai§ lî n'dai. I took boat this.	This is the boat which I took.
Ngai'fê thâ'dai§ sing'pho. Me threatened man.	The man that abused me.
Châ'dai‖ lî. Grounded boat.	The boat that grouuded.
Nyê'nâ la-gong'goi jû'dai§ My leg in pierced ma'sôn la'bû kâp'hâ. "pangi" poisoned.	The "panji" that pierced my foot (was) poisoned.

* "Dûm-shûn'dai" is a verbal noun.

† "Lû" "and" "khât" are the bare roots of verb, but are used to express the present and future tenses, *vide* page 31 *ante*.

‡ The participial "dai" connects the verb with the noun, and is equivalent to our relative pronoun.

§ Participial construction. The particle in "dai" connects the verb with the noun, and is equivalent to our relative pronoun.

Interrogative Pronouns.

Lam da'mâ' choi *	Road who knows?	Who knows the road?
Da'mâ wâ gâp'dai ? †	Who pig shot?	Who shot the pig?
Ngai da-mâ'fê sû ? ‡	I who to speak?	To whom shall I speak?
Nâng'fê ga-dê'na-wâ″ thâ'dai ?†	You which (man) abused?	Which (man) abused you?
Nâng gi'ning dî'hâ ?	You what manner did?	How did you do it?
Khî nâng'fê gining'dî dûp ?*	He you what manner strike?	How did he strike you?
Nâng gi'ning sot san'dai§ lî râ'dai?	You what sort boat require?	What kind of a boat do you want?
Lî ga'dê sâ'dai?	Boat how many came?	How many boats came.
Nâ'nâ n'gâ ga'dê ngâ'dai ?	Your land now much is?	How much land have you?
Nâng ga-dê'lâng khî'fê mû ?‖	You how many times him see?	How often have you seen him?
Nâ¶ ming ma-khai'mâ ?	Your name what?	What (is) your name?
N'dai ma-khai'mâ ?	This what?	What (is) this?
Nâng ga-dê'goi sâ'dai ?	You where to going'?	Where are you going to?
Nâng ga-loi'mê khî'fê mû'dai ?**	You when him seeing ?	When did you see him ?

Demonstrative Pronouns.

Sing'pho n'dai nâ'pháng.	Man this deaf.	This man (is) deaf.
Ngâ'shan n'dai ga'jâ	Fish this good.	This fish (is) good.
N'dai nâ¶ ning-nau'î″ ?††	This your sister ?	Is this your sister ?

---

* "Choi" and "dûp" are the mere roots of the verb ; the first is used to denote present, and the second past time, *vide* page 31 *ante.*

† "Gâp'dai" and "thâ'dai" are in the present tense used to denote past time, *vide* page 31 *ante.*

‡ "Sû," root of verb used to express future tense, *vide* page 31 *ante.*

§ "Sot san'dai," or "sotrai'dai," *lit.*, what being kind.

‖ "Mû" mere root of verb, used to denote past time, *vide* page 31 *ante.*

¶ "Nâ" is often used in lieu of "nâ'nâ" the full form of the possessive.

** Present tense used to denote past time.

†† Interrogative "î" tacked directly on to the noun.

M'bâ n'dai ô'râ phâ n'rê. Cloth this that like not.	This cloth is not like that one.
N'dai bok nâ ning-shâ'ï″ ?* These your children ?	Are these your children ?
Sing'pho sî'dai bok'fô cha'rû jo'û. Men those to liquor give.	Give those men liquor.
M'bâ sî'dai ga'grî kâp'dai. Cloth that dirty is.	That cloth is dirty.
Lî sî'dai gû'man. Boat that empty.	That boat (is) empty.
Sing'pho sî'dai mî pai'ï″†? Man that blind ?	Is that man blind ?
Bai'nam sî'dai bok nâ-nâ'ï″† ? Goats those yours ?	Are those goats yours ?
Sing'pho sî'dai bok da'lâ tsî jô'û. Men those rupees ten give.	Give those men ten rupees.

11, 12, 13, 14, 16, 17.—Verbs.

Ngai shan mû'dai. I deer see.	I see a deer.
Ngai ding'lâ tai'dai. I old (man) become am.	I am aged.
Dai'ni shi'bâ ka-thet dai. To-day very hot is.	It is very hot to-day.
Khâ n'dai jân'prû ma'ga yông'dai. River this east direction flows.	This river flows easterly.
Ma'râng thû'dai. Raining is.	It is raining.
Dai'nî m'bûng‡ n'bung'dai. To-day wind not blowing.	There is no wind to-day.
Nam that'dai. Jungle thick is.	The jungle is thick.
Khî shat sî-dû'dai. She rice cooking is.	She is cooking rice.
Khî shat sî-dû'ï″§ ? She rice cooking ?	Is she cooking rice ?
Gui sî nong hâ.‖ Dog died quite has.	The dog is quite dead.
Nâng sing'pho'ï″ §? You Singpho ?	Are you a Singpho ?
Ngai ô-râ'goi khrû yâ ngâ'hâ. I there six days remained.	I was six days there.

---

* Interrogative "ï" tacked directly on to the noun.

† Interrogative "ï," the first tacked on to an adjective, the second on to a pronoun, *vide* page 45 *ante*.

‡ "M'bûng bûng"=blow. This sentence might be turned thus:—"dai'nî m'bûng n'ngâ" = there is no wind to day.

§ Interrogative "ï."

‖ Past tense suffix tacked on to an adverb, *vide* page 45 *ante*.

Ma'nî ngai ma-chî'dai. * Yesterday I ill am.	Yesterday I was ill.
Sing'pho bok phrong'hâ. (The) men ran away.	The men ran away.
Mi-ling'goi shan khâng mât'hâ. Forest in deer tracks lost.	I lost the deer's tracks in the forest.
Khî hât'goi sâ'dai.* He "hát" to gone.	He has gone to the "hát.'
Ngai shan krâ'hâ I deer hit.	I hit the deer.
Khî khî'fe n'khong'lâng yû sâ'dai * He him twice see (to) went.	He went twice to see him.
Da-lâ'mâ wû ma'sûm ma-rî'hâ. Rupee one fowls three bought.	I bought three fowls for one rupee.
Ngai la'khon aî'mâ thâ lû'hâ. I bracelet one found.	I have found a bracelet.
Nyê'nâ si'nat ma-lî'lâng gâp'hâ. My gun four times fired.	I fired my gun four times.
Ngai khî'fê n'dûp'dai. I him not beat.	I did not beat him.
Ngai m'pho'nî bai'wâ. I to-morrow return.	I (will) return to-morrow.
Khî nâng'fe da'lâ n'khong jô'â. He you rupees two give will.	He will give you two rupees.
Gûm-râng'î† nâng'fê la-khât'â. Horse you kick will.	The horse will kick you.
Yû jûng khû nan n'prû'â. Rat hole from not emerge will.	The rat will not come out of the hole.
Khâ'î† ning'gâm gî'â. River bank break will.	The river will break the bank.
Ngai dê'ning Hû-kong'goi sâ'â. I next year Hukong to go will.	I will go to Hukong next year.
Nâng wû n'dai bok ma-rî'î"‡ ? You fowls these buy?	Will you buy these fowls?
Ngai phûn lûng ngût'â. I tree climb able.	I can climb a tree.
Ngai phûn lûng n'ngût'â. I tree climb unable.	I cannot climb a tree.
Nâng phûn lûng ngût-â' khâ". You tree climb able?	Can you climb a tree.
Shan mû-hâ'khâ" khî'fê san'û. Deer seen have? him ask.	Ask him if he saw any deer.
Dai'nî sâ-yâng'gâ phrâng'nî dû'â. To-day going if day after morrow arrive will.	If I start to-day, I will arrive the day after to-morrow.

* Present tense used to denote past time.
† Nominatival "î," denoting agent.
‡ Interrogative "î."

Nâng phûn'goi n'la-gan' yâng"gâ You tree in not hiding if shan'î* mû'â. deer see will.	If you don't get up the tree, the deer will see (you).
Shan'wâ† mû-dî'gâ gâp dî gâ ai'hâ. Deer seeing shooting well.	Had he seen the deer, he would have shot it.
Ga'lau la-gat'û. Quickly run.	Run quickly.
N'dai pôn'û. This lift.	Lift this.
Shî'yâ kring'î‡ sâ'û. Ten days staying go.	Come here ten days hence.
Sing-pho'wâ lup'û. Man bury.	Bury the man.
Ngai chû sâ§ krit'â. I alone go fear will.	I am afraid to go alone.
Nâng kû'wâ lâ§ ma'lâp yâng gâ You bamboos bring forget if ngai pot'â. I angry will.	If you forget to bring the bamboos, I will be angry.
Khî n'gû ma'rî§ sâ'dai. He rice buy going.	He is going to buy rice.
Khûm ma sû'û. Don't lie.	Don't tell a lie.
Ngai nâng'fê jô-a'jo lâ'dai‖. I you to give to brought.	I brought it to give you.
Si'lui dê'yâng nyê lî'ûng Lime picking while my finger jû'î¶ jû'hâ. thorn by pricked.	While picking the lime, I pricked my finger.
Khâ rap-da'goi** (*or* rap-yâng'î) River crossing on lî khûp'hâ. boat upset.	While crossing the river, the boat upset.
Ngai ma-chî'dî ngâ'yâng†† shâ n'ngûtâ. I ill being when eat unable.	When I am ill, I cannot eat.

* Nominatival "î" denoting agent.

† This is the "wâ" alluded to at page 5 *ante*.

‡ The participial suffix "dî" is occasionally shortened to "î" thus "kring'î"="kring'dî."

§ "Sâ," "lâ," and "ma'ri" are the mere roots of the verbs used for the infinitive.

‖ Present tense used to denote past time, *vide* page 31 *ante*.

¶ "Î" instrumental postposition.

** "Rap-da'goi" is a verbal noun, with the locative case postposition tacked on. The "dai" is contracted to "da" for sake of euphony.

†† "Ma-chî'dî ngâ'yâng" = compound verb, "ma'chî" is an adjective = ill, with the participial suffix "dî" attached, and "ngâ" is the substantive verb, *vide* page 40 *ante*.

Phûn la'khûng dan-da'goi* khî krat'hâ. Bough cutting in he fell.	While cutting the branch, he fell.
Tsî'rong mû'dî ngai phrong'hâ. Tiger seeing I fled.	Seeing the tiger I ran away.
Li-goi'nâ† n'chin got'dî nyê'nâ rai Boat water bailing my things bâng'û. load up.	Bail out the boat, and put my things in it.
Nâng sing-oi'î ma-sû'dî ngai You before lying I n'yûm'â. not believe will.	You spoke falsely before, I will not believe you.
Wâ krâ-da'goi‡ gî-vin'ha. Pig hitting on turned round.	The pig, being hit, turned round.
Shan phî wâ§ gâ'dî kâ-shin'û. Deer skin strip wash.	Having skinned the deer, wash the skin.
Phûn wâ§ ga-nôn'û. Tree shake.	Shake the tree.
Khî'î‖ ngai'fê tsî-mai'hâ. He me cured.	He has cured me.
Nyê'nâ ken'sû wâ§ khî'î‖ tsî-mât'hâ. My cow he lost.	He has lost my cow.
Ngai nâng'fê Sing'pho gâ tsî-rin'gâ. I you Singpho language teach will.	I will teach you Singpho.
Shan wâ§ khân-a'jo sâ tsî-nûn'û. Deer track to go cause.	Tell him to track the deer.
M'bâ wâ§ bai-lâ'û. Cloth take back.	Take back the cloth.
Sing'pho ô-râ'wâ shan mû kûn n'mû'hâ khi'fê sâ'dî san'û.	Go and ask that man if he has seen a deer.
Ngai yâ ga-lai'mang ning'gûm tai'hâ. I now again strong become.	I am now strong again.
Ngai nam'taî wâ dep¶ n'ngût'â. I fruit reach unable.	I cannot reach the fruit.

18. Adverbs.

Sing'pho bok rau pru'dai.** Singphos together appearing.	The Singphos came together.

* "Dan-da'goi" is a verbal noun with the locative case post-position tacked on. The "dai" is contracted to "da" for sake of euphony.

† One would suppose that "lî'nâ n'chin" explains the meaning as well as "lî-goi'nâ."

‡ "Krada'goi" is a verbal noun, with "goi" added.

§ The "wâ" is either used as an expletive, or it takes the place of the English demonstrative pronoun *it*, for instance "phûn wâ ga-nôn'û" I take to mean "tree *it* shake."

‖ These "î" denote the agent.

¶ Mere root of verb used for infinitive, *vide* page 34, *ante*.

** Present tense used to denote past time, *vide* page 31 *ante*.

Ngai'fê n'dai thêng yâ* kûn sî'dai Me this much give or that thêng yâ*? much give?	Will you give me this much or that much?
Chau'sû sâ'û nyê la'gông ma-chî'dai.† Slowly go my leg sore.	Go slowly, my foot is sore.
Mî'phrâp ka'prip yâng phûn ka-tâ'î Lightning while tree beneath phûng dûng'û. don't sit.	Don't sit under a tree while it is lightning.
Dai-ning'î‡ î'na mâm ga'jâ mang ga'jâ This year in our dhan good and good n'ga'jâ mang n'ga'jâ. not good and not good.	Our dhan (crop) is neither good nor bad this year.
Khî'nâ n'tâ ma'rêng khâ-âng'î‡. His house village middle in.	His house is in the middle of the village.
Nyê'nâ nûm'shâ§ ma-chî'dî dai'dî My wife ill being therefore ngai sâ n'ngût'hâ. I go unable.	My wife is ill, therefore I cannot go.
Nâng ai rai'dî ning'kin choi â'î‖? You well sing know?	Can you sing well?
N'dai sot di'dî mûng'lî diû. This wise doing work do.	Do the work in this way.
Ma'reng wâ bûm ka-tâ'î‡ ngâ. Village hill below is.	The village is below the hill.
Ma'reng wa la-thâ'î‡ ngâ. Village upstream is.	The village is upstream.

MISCELLANEOUS PHRASES.

TRAVEL.

Ma'ning ngai Tel'pûng¶ goi'nau sâ'dî Last year I Margherita from going Ning-râng'nong goi dû'hâ Ningrangnong to reached sî'dai goi nan Patkoi bûm thence Patkoi mountain lau rai'dî Nâm'yûng** gâ dû'ha. crossing Namyûng reached.	Last year I marched from Margherita to Ningrangnong; thence to Namyung across the Patkoi.

* "Yâ," root of verb give, used to denote present tense, *vide* page 31 *ante*.

† "Ma'chî" means *any* bodily ailment.

‡ "Î" locative case postposition.

§ "Nyê'nâ nûm'shâ" means, *lit.*, my woman. Singphos have no word for wife.

‖ "Î" interrogative particle.

¶ Margherita is almost always spoken of as Telpung, owing to the oil springs in its neighbourhood.

** "Gâ," probably derived from "ma'gâ" = place, spot, &c., means neighbourhood.

Sâ'hêb n'khong ngai da'pham Sahebs two I with nâng'dai*. accompanied.	Two Sahebs accompanied me.
Nâm'yûng ma'rêng ka-chi'dai Namyung village small is thing'gong (*or* n'tâ) ma'chat chû. houses eight only.	Namyung is a small village (it has) only eight houses.
Â-ghî'nâ ming'gâ† Pû'sâjauwan. Headman's name Pusajauwan.	The headman's name is Pusajauwan.
Khi'gâ† Pu'sâ phan. He Pusa clan.	He is of the Pusa clan.
Si'dai ma-rêng'nâ sing'pho yong That village of people all ma-chân'dai. poor are.	The people of that village are all poor.
N'dûng ma'gâ ngâ'dai‡ Kha'khângbok South side dwelling Nágas sing'pho thau'dî§ nat human beings sacrificing spirits jô'dai. give.	The Nágas on the south side of the Patkoi are human sacrificers.
Thûng n'dai li-ning'mê n'rai'â‖. Custom this yearly not be will.	The custom is not a yearly one.
Khi'nî nat jô'yâng Kha'khâng They spirits giving when Nágas yong khûm'dî lû shâ pî-ô'dai¶ all collecting drink food feast ga'lâng** ga'lâng gâ thau'dai sometimes sacrificed sing'pho nûm'chân goi'nan person distance from ma'rî†† lû'dai ga'lâng purchasing obtained are some- ga'lâng gâ phen khât'dî lû'dai. times battling obtained are.	When the ceremony takes place, all the Nágas collect, and sometimes the victims are purchased from a distance, sometimes they are seized in battle.

---

* Present tense used to denote past time, *vide* page 31 of grammar.

† "Ming"=name, "gâ" is merely an expletive, with "ming" and "khî."

‡ "Ngâ'dai" is a verbal noun.

§ "Thau" means *lit.* to cut in two.

‖ "N'rai"=substantive verb "rai" with negative particle "n'" prefixed. The "â" is the future tense suffix.

¶ "Lû shâ pîôdai" means to *feast*, *i.e.*, enjoy eating and drinking.

** "Ga'lâng" is the adverbial numeral *once*, *vide* page 15 of grammar.

†† "Ma'rî"=purchase, "lû"=obtain.

Khâng n'dai bok î* wâ lô lô rêm'dai Nágas these pigs many keep ken'sû mang ngá mang wû cows also buffaloes also fowls mang rêm'dai. also keep.	These Nágas keep numerous pigs, also cows, buffaloes, and fowls.
Khî-nî'nâ n'tâ kû'wâ da'pham gâp'dai Their houses bamboos with built ma'chat† shi'bat ngâ'dai. untidy are.	Their houses are made of bamboo, and are very dirty.
Sing'pho gâ n'kau'gâ‡ choi Singpho language some know n'kau'gâ n'choi. some not know.	Some know Singpho, some don't.
Khî-nî'nâ nûm'shâ bok n'phrâ-phrû'dai. Their women not comely are.	Their women are not pretty.
Khî'nî vî mûng'lî yông dî'dai. They field work all do.	They do all the field work.
Nûm'shâ lâ'shâ râm-râm'dî gûn§ Women men equally load carry ngût'dai. able are.	They can carry as heavy a load as the men.
Lâ'shâ bok kâ'nî‖ lû'dai nûm'shâ bok Males opium smoke females n'lû'dai‖. not smoke.	The males smoke opium (but) the females do not.
Ning'then ning'khâ thû'dai nûm'shâ Lip chin tatooed woman ai'mâ chû ngai mû'dai¶. one only I saw.	I saw only one woman tattooed; on the lip and chin.
Ngai bûm'goi ngâ'yâng khûn I hills in staying while twenty ma'chat yâ ma'râng thû'hâ. eight days rain fell.	It rained for 28 days while I was in the hills.

---

* Nominatival "î" denoting the agent.

† "Ma'chat shi'bat" is a colloquial saying, meaning untidy.

‡ "Kau" *or* "n'kau" means literally half, one portion, &c.

§ "Ma'gûn"=a load, "ma'gûn gûn"=carry a load, "Ma'gûn" is here understood.

‖ "Lû" is the root of the verb to *drink*. Singphos have no single word for *smoke* in the English sense, so to express the meaning properly, one would have to say "lû'dî" (pipe), "pham'î" (*or* "da'pham'î") (by means of), "wan khût" (smoke), "lû" (draw into lungs).

¶ Present tense used to express past time, *vide* page 31 of grammar.

Ma'râng thû'dai* ning-khan'î lam Rain fallen on account of road shî'bâ ma-neu'dai† lûng‡ la'jâ‡. very slippery is climb difficult.	The rain made the roads very slippery and the climbing difficult.
Khân n'dai bok'î§ Hû'kong ma'sôn Nágas these Hukong near goi'nan ko'noi lô lô thû'dai. from rubber much cut.	A great deal of rubber is cut from the vicinity of Hukong by these Nágas.
Khî'nî chân-da'goi‖ sâ'dî ko'noi They far away going rubber thû'dai. cut.	They go long distances to cut it.
Khî'nî nat¶ jô'dai. They spirits offer.	They (are) spirit-worshippers.
Nat yông'goi ngâ'dai** ngû'dî Spirits everywhere dwelling saying khî'nî wât†† yû'dai. they oracles consult.	Being superstitious, they consult the oracles.
Khî-nî'nâ ma'rêng ai ai gâ‡‡ ga-bâ'- Their villages some large dai. are.	Some of their villages are large.
Khî-nî'nâ lû'dai§§ n'chin n'ga-jâ'- Their drinking water not good dî"‖‖mang ngai dû bong'dai¶¶ being even I goitred sing'pho n'mu'hâ. persons not saw.	Notwithstanding that their drinking water is bad, I saw no goitre.

---

* "Ma'râng thû'dai" = past participal passive of "marâng thû" = to rain.

† "Ma'neu" is an adverb, with present tense suffix attached to it.

‡ "Lûng" is the bare root of the verb to climb, used for the verbal noun, and "la'jâ" is an adjective without any tense suffix.

§ "Bok" is one of the particles denoting plurality, with the nominatival "î" attached to denote the agent.

‖ This is the participial suffix "dai" tacked on to an adverb and shortened to "da" for sake of euphony.

¶ "Nat" is apparently used here for the dative case.

** "Ngâ'dai" is here used as a verbal noun, meaning dwelling, or existing, *vide* page 37 of grammar.

†† "Wât yû" means to consult the oracle by means of a bamboo heated in the fire.

‡‡ "Ai ai" means, literally, one one.

§§ "Lû'dai" = verbal noun.

‖‖ "Ga'-jâ" = good, "n'ga-ja'" = not good. The "dî" is the participial suffix tacked on to the adjective, "n'ga-ja'dî" = therefore "not being good."

¶¶ "Dû" = neck, "bong" = swell.

Phên prû'yâng gâ lam'î* ma'sôn War starting when road on panjis jûn-a'î"† ? fix will ?	When at war, do they "panji" their paths ?
Ma'rêng prâ‡ sâ-yâng'gâ gin'ing Village attack going when what rai'dai lai prâ‡ sâ'dai§ ? kind custom attack go ?	What is their custom when attacking a village ?
Khî'nî gûm'dî sâ kûn ga-rû'dî‖ They stooping go or yelling sâ¶ ? go ?	Do they creep up or rush at it yelling ?
Daffa-nong'nâ ma'rêng bûm'goi kûn Daffanong's village hills in or lî'yang î** ? plains ?	Is Daffanong's village in the hills or in the plains ?
Hû'kong mûng'î yong'a n'la Hukong country in all than ga-bâ' grau'dai khî-î"†† ? greatest he ?	Is he the biggest (man) in the Hukong country ?
Hû'kong mûng'î ngâ'dai Sing'pho Hukong country in dwelling Singphos Khê mûng'î sâ kûn ? China country to go or (not) ?	Do the Hukong Singphos visit China ?
Khê bok Hû-kong'î ma'khai‡‡ ma'khai Chinese Hukong to what what nou'dai ? carry ?	What do the Chinese bring into Hukong ?
Hû'kong goi'nan ma'khai ma'khai Hukong from what lâ'dai ? take ?	What do they take from it ?

---

* "Î" = locative case postposition.

† "Î" = interrogative particle.

‡ Here "prâ," the bare root of the verb, is used for the infinitive *vide* page 34 of grammar.

§ No interrogative particle used, because "gin'ing rai'dai", sufficiently denotes interrogation.

‖ "Ga'rû" is the peculiar diabolical row made by Singphos when rushing to attack.

¶ "Sâ" is the bare root of the verb used here for the present tense, *vide* page 31 grammar.

** This may be either the locative case postposition, or the interrogative particle. I think it is the former.

†† Interrogative "î."

‡‡ Interrogative pronouns and adverbs are sometimes repeated for the sake of emphasis.

Khi'nî li-ning'mê Hû-kong'î sâ kûn*? They yearly Hukong to visit?	Do they visit Hukong yearly?
Â-ghî'nâ â'khâng lû kûn*? Headmen's orders get?	By permission of the chiefs?
Hû'kong singpho'î† khi-ni'fê râ‡ Hukong people them desire kûn n'râ‡? or not desire?	Do the Hukong people desire them?
Khi'nî khi-nî'fê krit‡ kûn n'krit‡? They them fear or not fear?	Do they fear them?
Khê sing'pho Sing'pho gâ choi‡ Chinese Singpho language know kûn n'choi‡? or not know?	Do the Chinese know Singpho?
Khê sing'pho si'nat yon yám‡ dût Chinese guns both powder sell kûn n'dût‡? or not sell?	Do the Chinese sell powder and guns to the Singphos?
Sing'pho â'ghî khê chau-phâ'fê Singpho headmen Chinese king lâk'shong yâ kûn n'yâ? tribute give or not give?	Do the Hukong chiefs pay tribute to China?
Mûng'khôm gâ gâ§ Mân gâ. Mainkhwom Burmese territory kûn Sing'pho gâ? or Singpho territory?	Is Mainkhwom Singpho country or Burmese?
Sûm-boi'ya"nong do'mâ? Somboianong who?	Who is Somboianong?
Phen khât-yâng'î lûk'shûk. Fighting in followers (armed followers) ga-dê'mâ tsi'khûm ngûtâ? how many collect able will be?	How many fighting men can he collect?

COMPLAINT.

Nâng ma-khai'mâ râ? You what require?	What do you want?

---

* "Kûn" is an interrogative particle, expressing uncertainty or doubt.

† Nominatival "î" denoting agent.

‡ These are the bare roots of the verbs used for the present tense, *vide* page 70 of grammar.

§ *Vide* foot-note, page 31, where meaning of "gâ" is explained; "gâ" is merely an expletive, or it takes the place of the English demonstrative pronoun *it*.

‖ "Phen khat" means *to wage* or *carry on*.

Jau'wê* nyê mî'yam ai'mâ phrong- Sir my slave one run away hâ'dai tsî·bai'yâ"dî† ni'yâ. has returning well.	Sir! one of my slaves has run away, I wish you to have (him) returned (to me).
Khî nyê'nâ sî'nat mang la'gû,‡ rai He my gun also stolen things ga'leng mang shi'bâ la-gû'hâ. other also many stolen.	He has stolen my gun and many other things.
Mûng§nûm-dû'î mî'yam rêm ‖ Empress slaves keep n'ngû'dai ning·khân'î nâ-nâ not allowing because your phrong'dai mî'yamwâ ga-rim'dî fled slave seizing bai'yâ n'ngût'â. return unable.	(I) cannot compel the man the man to return to you, as our Empress does not countenance slavery.
Bai'yâ n'ngût'dî mang ¶ ngai Return unable being even I khî'fê tsî gâ ** lâ'dî san'gâ. him calling ask will.	(But) although I cannot return him, I will have him fetched and interrogate him.
Nâ†† mî-am'î‡‡ si'nat mang rai Your slave gun and things ga'leng mang lâ'hâ sû ngût-yâng'gâ others also taken speakable being ngai si'dai bai-yâ'â. I them return will.	If you can prove that he has stolen your gun and other goods, I will return them.
Mî'yam n'dai'nâ§§ manû kum'phrong Slave this price rupees la'cha bau n'khong si'nat ai'mâ hundred gongs two gun one dai'thêng khî'fê bai'yâ‖‖ n'gnût· this much him return unable yâng'gâ khî'nâ ma'nû bai'yâ‖‖ râ. being his price return necessary.	This man cost me Rs. 100, two gongs, and one gun. If therefore you cannot return him, you must make good his cost.

---

* "Jau" *or* "jau'wê" is always used by an *inferior* when addressing a *superior*.

† "Bai'yâ" means to return, give back, and the "tsi" prefixed to it means *to cause* (to be given back) *vide* page 41 of grammar.

‡ "La'gû" is the bare root used to denote past time, *vide* page 31 of grammar.

§ "Mûng nûm'dû" means *lit.* owner of the country. The "î" suffixed is the nominative particle denoting the agent.

‖ "Rêm" is the root of the verb used for the infinitive, *vide* page 34 of grammar.

¶ "Bai'yâ n'ngût dî mang" means *although unable to return.*

** "Tsi'gâ lâ'dî" is a compound verb, meaning to cause to be present, call and bring.

†† "Nâ" is here used for the possessive, *vide* page 16 of grammar.

‡‡ Nominatival "î" denoting agent.

§§ "Nâ" is the possessive suffix attached to the demonstrative pronoun; "mî'yam n'dai'nâ"=this slave.

‖‖ "Bai'yâ" is the root, used here for the infinitive.

Ngai n'ngût'â ngai khî'fê n'tsî' I unable will be I him not made phrong'hâ* sî-dai'dî khî'nâ mâ'nû (him) fly therefore his price nâng'fê bai'yâ thûng n'ngâ'dai. you to return custom not exist.	I cannot do so. I did not induce the man to bolt, and therefore it is not our custom to pay ransom.
N'dai nâ mî'yam rai-â'î"?† This your slave is?	Is this your slave?
Khî mûng'nûn gâ choi-â'khâ"? He Assamese language understands?	Does he understand Assamese?
N'choi'â. Not understand.	No.
Ngai khî'fê Sing'pho gâ'î‡ I him to Singpho language in sû'â. speak will.	I will speak to him in Singpho.
Nâ ming ma-khai'mâ? Your name what?	What (is) your name?
Nyê ming Nong. My name Nong.	My name (is) Nong.
Sing'pho n'dai sû'dai nang khî'nâ Man this says you his mî'yâm rai'dai nâng khî'nâ si'nat slave are you his gun mang§ la'gû rai ga'leng mang also stole things other also la-gû'hâ. stole.	This man says you are his slave, and have stolen his gun and other things.
Ngai khî'na mî'yam rai'dai khî nong I his slave am he al- nong dûp'dai ning-khân'î ngai ways beating because I phong'hâ khî'nâ si'nat mang rai fled his gun and things ga'gâ mang n'la-gû'hâ. other also not stole.	I am his slave. I ran away because he was always beating (me). (I) did not steal his gun and other goods.
Nâ‖ la-tâ'î‡ si'nat ngâ'dai da'mâ Your hand in gun being whose si'nat? gun?	Whose gun have you in your hand?

* "Phrong" means to flee, run away, "tsî'phrong" to cause to flee, induce to flee, and "n'tsî'phrong"=not cause to flee.

† "Rai'â"=will be. The "î" tacked on to it is the interrogative particle.

‡ "Î" locative case postpositions.

§ "La'gû" is the root, used here to denote past time, *vide* page 31 of grammar.

‖ "Nâ" is here used for the possessive case.

Nyê'nâ rai'dai ngai ma-ri'hâ. Mine is I purchased (it).	It is mine. (I) purchased it.
Kûm'phrong ga-dê'goi lû'hâ? Money where obtained?	Where did (you) get the money from?
N'khong ning lo'hâ ngai ken'sû ai'ma Two years ago I cow one dût'hâ kûm'phrong khûn sold money (rupee) twenty lû'hâ n'dai si'nat ma-ri'hâ si'nat obtained this gun purchased gun n'dai khî'nâ rai-yâng'gâ da'ma da'ma this his being if who who choi'dai tsî'gâ* sî-nûn'û. knows call cause (him to).	Two years ago I sold a cow for Rs. 20, and purchased this gun (with the money). If this is his gun, let him call people to prove it.
Si'nat n'dai sing-gan'î† rai gâ'leng Gun this besides things other mang non-hâ'khâ"? also brought?	Did (you) bring anything else besides this gun?
Nâng lam'î gi-ning'dî shâ You road on how food lû-hâ'dai? obtained?	How did you obtain food on the road?
Ngai n'gû non'dai‡ shâ§ n'lo'hâ I rice brought eat not sufficed sî-dai'dî phî'dî shâ'hâ. therefore begging fed.	I brought rice (with me), (but it) did not suffice, therefore I begged food.
Nâng ga-dê'goi yup hâ'dai? You where slept?	Where did you sleep.
Ngai sing-oi'î n'khong yâ ching-nî'î I first on two days day time in phûn'î lûng'dî la-gan'dî‖ ngâ'hâ tree in climbing hid sî-nâ'î sâ'hâ. night in travelled.	The first two days I hid in a tree, (and) travelled at night.
Nâng sî-nâ'î sâ-yâng'î You night in travelling on n'krit-hâ'khâ"? not frightened?	Were you not afraid to travel at night?
Ngai sî'râ si'nat ngâ'hâ. I with gun possessed.	I had a gun with me.
Nâng shat ga-loi'mê sî-dû'hâ? You food when cooked?	When did you cook food?

---

* "Tsî'gâ"=root, here used for infinitive.

† "Sin-gan'î" means *lit.* on the outside.

‡ Present tense used to denote past time.

§ "Shâ"=root used for infinitive.

‖ "La-gân'dî ngâ'hâ" is a compound verb, meaning *lit.* "hiding stayed," *vide* page 42 of grammar.

<table>
<tr><td>Ngai'fê khân-da'wâ bok'î* wan khût
Me trackers smoke
mû'dî nyê ngâ'dai shîrâ choi'â
seeing my hiding place know will
krit'dî ngai shat n'sî-dû'hâ.
fearing I food not cooked.</td><td>I did not cook lest my fire should discover my whereabouts to my pursuers.</td></tr>
<tr><td>Nâng'fê khân'dai ngû'dî nâng gi-
You tracking saying you
ning'dî choi'hâ?
how knew?</td><td>How did you know you were being pursued?</td></tr>
<tr><td>Yong yong phrong'dai mî'yam†
All runaway slaves
khân'dai.
tracked are.</td><td>All runaway slaves are pursued.</td></tr>
<tr><td>Khân'dai sing-pho'î‡ nâng'fê ga-rim'-
Trackers you caught-
dî gâ nâng gin'ing dî?§
had you what do?</td><td>If your pursuers had caught you, what would you have done?</td></tr>
<tr><td>Ngai si-nut'î¶ gâp'â.
I gun by shoot would.</td><td>I would have shot them.</td></tr>
<tr><td>Nâng ga-dê'goi ngâ‖ mit'dai?
You where stay wish?</td><td>Where do you wish to live?</td></tr>
<tr><td>Nâng jau'wê â'khâng yâ'dai ma-gâ'î
You sir order giving place in
ngâ-â'mâ.
stay will.</td><td>I will stay wherever it pleases your honour to order me to.</td></tr>
<tr><td>Khâ ô'râ kran'î ngâ râ'dai.
River that side on dwell must.</td><td>You must live on the other side of the river.</td></tr>
<tr><td>Ai'yâ nâng jau'wê mit rê.
Very well you sir wish (it) verily.</td><td>Very well. It is your honour's wish.</td></tr>
<tr><td>Messâkî gâ'î** Dwan'yâ ât'â.
Messaki at Dwanyas many.</td><td>There are numerous Dwanyas at Messaki.</td></tr>
</table>

---

* "Khân-da'wâ bok'î"="khân," root of verb "to track," with participial "dai" shortened to "da" for sake of euphony, and explotive "wâ" attached, meaning "trackers." "Bok" is simply a particle of plurality, and the "î" is the nominatival "î" denoting the agent.

† "Phrong'dai mî'yam." This is a participial construction. The "dai" connects the verb with the noun, and is equivalent to our relative pronoun.

‡ "Khân'dai sing-pho'î"=the same; properly translated, this would mean by the tracking persons, or trackers.

§ "Dî" is the bare root of the verb.

¶ Instrumental "î."

‖ "Ngâ" root used for infinitive.

** "Gâ" from "ma'gâ"=place, spot, is used as a kind of locative suffix.

Nâ * n'tâ gâp† n'ngût ting-sâng'î‡ Your house erect not able until Dwan'yâ sî'râ ngâ'û. Dwanyas with remain.	Stay with the Dwanyas until you can erect a house.
Khî'nâ mi'yam ngâ-yâng'î (*or* tai'dî§ His slave being while becoming ngâ-yâng'î) ma'khai mûng'lî¶ when what work rai'dai ? performed ?	What work did you perform while his slave ?
Ngai mûng'lî ga'gâ ga'gâ lo lo dî'hâ. I work different many performed.	I performed many different works.
Nâng lî sî'gâ† choi-â'khâ" ? You boat paddle understand ?	Can you paddle a boat ?
Nyê shat sî-dû'dai n'dî n'ngâ'dai. My food cooking pot not exists.	I have no pot for cooking.
Nyai ai'mâ yâ'gâ. I one give will.	I will give you one.
Nyê'nâ m'bâ mang n'ngâ. My cloth also not exists.	I have no cloth either.
Ngai nâng'fê rai ga'leng yâ I you things other give n'ngût'â. unable.	I cannot give you anything more.
Nâng n'gû n'jô'yang"gâ ngai kâ'si‖ You rice not giving if I starving sî'â. die will.	If you don't give me rice, I shall starve.

* "Nâ" is used here for the possessive case.

† "Gâp" and "sî'gâ" are roots, used for the infinitive, *vide* page 34 of grammar.

‡ "Ting-sâng'î" may be construed "interval in," the "î" is the locative case postposition.

§ "Tai'dî ngâ" is a compound verb, *vide* page 42 of grammar.

¶ Present tense used to denote past time, *vide* page 31 of grammar.

‖ "Kâ'sî" is an adjective meaning *hungry*. It is used here in its root form, as a past participle, namely, instead of "kâ'sî'dî," *vide* page 31 of grammar.

VOCABULARY.

VOCABULARY.

In the following Vocabulary I have given the roots only of verbs. There is no complete formal distinction between nouns, adjectives, and verbs. Each in its root is indistinguishable from the others, for instance, "khân," a noun, means a mark left by something passing; "khân" with the imperative particle suffixed means, track, follow by traces, or footsteps; "lûp" is used as a noun, meaning a grave, and likewise as a root verb, meaning to bury; "pûp" is a kiss, and also *to kiss*; "yêt" is an adjective, meaning decomposed, rotten, and is likewise used as a verb, "ning'shin," dark, night, is either a noun or adjective, &c., &c.

English.	Singpho.	Remarks.
Accompany, attend, escort, go with, *v.*	Nâng.	
Abduct, *v.*	Sing'yên.	"Sin'yen" means more to *snatch*, "ning-gûn'î lâ" = by force take, also expresses the meaning.
About (on the point of) *adv.*	Qui.	
Able (also means accomplish, finish) *a.*	Ngût.	
Above (in a higher place) *adv.*	Ning-sâng'î (ning-tsâng'î.)	The "î" is the locative case postposition. Above, *in addition to*, is "la thâ'î"
Abuse, *v.*	Ma'châ.	
Acid, *a.*	Khri.	
Adze, *n.*	Ning'wâ.	Same as axe.
Afterwards, subsequently, *adv.*	Ning-dim'î.	"Yet" which means soon, just now, &c., and is equivalent to the Assamese word "â-tho'nî kôê'" is also used to define indefinite future time, so is "m'phot," though the the latter is used for a somewhat remoter future.
Again, once more, *adv.*	Yâ mang, ga'lai mang.	
Ago, past, gone, *adv.* or *a.*	Lô.	

English.	Singpho.	Remarks.
Alike, equal in quantity, quality, or degree, *adv.*	Ai'mâ sot.	One kind, sort.
Alive	Khrûng.	
Almost, nearly, well nigh, *adv.*	Ga noi'hê.	"Qui"=about, &c., also used. In fact, the two words appear to be interchangeable.
Alone, only, singly, *a.*	Chû.	
Also, likewise, even, *conj.*	Mang.	
All, *a.*	Yông.	Generally repeated for emphasis.
All right (very well)	Ai'yâ.	Used elliptically.
Alligator	Gui'gai.	
Always, *adv.*	Nong.	
Amber, *n.*	Pat.	
Among, between, amidst, *prep.*	La-pân'î.	Also means in the interval, between such a time.
And, also, even, *conj.*	Mang.	
Anger, *n.*	Mi'sin pôt.	
Another, not the same, *a.*	Ga'gâ *or* ga'lai mang.	"Ga'gâ" means different.
Ant, *n.*	Gi'gin *or* gû'gin.	
Anus, *n.*	Chi'tin khû.	"Khû"=hole.
Approximately, *adv.*	M'phû *or* mâ.	"Mâ" is a particle expressing ambiguity.
Arm, hand, *n.*	La'tâ.	
Forearm, *n.*	La tâ la'phûm.	
Armpit, *n.*	Ka'phâ khû.	
Arrive at, reach, come, get to, &c., *v.*	Dû.	
Arrow, *n.*	Pa'lâ.	
Ask, inquire of, interrogative, *v.*	San.	
Assamese (native of Assam), *n.*	Mûng nûn sing'pho.	
At, *prep.*	*Made by* goi *or* î.	
Awaken, *v.*	Yûp sî'rât *or* tsî rât.	
Bad, not good, evil, ill, wicked, *a.*	N'ga-jâ'.	"Ga-jâ'n'rê" = good is not.
Bachelor, *n.*	Sing'krâ.	
Back, *n.*	Sing'mâng.	
Bag, *n.*	M'phêng.	

English.	Singpho.	Remarks.
Bald, *a.*	Bông khân.	{ *Assamese names of* / *Singpho names of*
		Tâ'pû = Wâ'râ.
		Jâ'tî = Mai'sâng.
Bamboo, *n.*	Kû'wâ.	Kâ'kô = Wâ'pho.
		Bû-lû'kâ = Mai'sang nâm.
		Bôjâl = Ka'thân.
Bamboo "chunga" *n.*	Kû'wâ n'dûm.	
Bamboo strips for tying thatch with, called tongâl by Assamese, *n.*	Pa'lî.	
Bank, of river, *n.*	Khâning'gâm.	"Khâ"=river.
Bark, *v.*	Wau.	
Bark of tree, *n.*	Phûn phî.	
Basket (carried on shoulder by means of a yoke) by men, *n.*	Shong'phai.	The wooden yoke in use is not unlike those used in England. It is called "ning'kau"." It has a plaited strap fastened at each end which goes over the carrier's head, so that it is carried partially by the yoke and partially by the head strap.
Basket, carried by means of a strap, on head, by women, *n.*	Shingnoi.	
Basket (small round one) *n.*	Mûng.	
Bat, *n.*	Pa'chip.	
Bathe, *v.*	Khâ'sin.	
Be, exist, &c., *v.*	Ngâ.	
Bead, *n.*	Ka'chî	"Î" shorter than one in word for small, chilly.
Beard, hair on chin, *n.*	Ning'khâ mûn.	"Ning'khâ"=chin.
Bear, *n.*	Chap.	
Bear, give birth to, produce, *v.*	Yû *or* Pâ.	They appear to be interchangeable, though the first is applied oftener to animals than the other. Nâng ga-dê'goi pâ'bâ / you where born. { Where were you born.

English.	Singpho.	Remarks.
Beat, strike, hit, *v.*	Dûp.	
Because, for this or that reason, on this account, *conj.*	Si'dai ning-khân'î.	
Beckon, *v.*	Wâk.	
Become, progress and transition into some other state, *v.*	Tai.	Nâng sing'pho You humanbeing tai'dai ga-dê'goi? became where? } Where were you born?
Bee, *n.*	La'gât.	Generic term.
Before, in front of, *prep.*	Sing-oi'î.	
Before, in time, previous, *adv.*	Sing oi'î.	"Mî"=just now, or some time previous, like the Assamese "â-thônî," and "Ma'lo" and "moi" are also used to denote previous indefinite time. "Ma'lo" means some days, and "moi" a long while previous.
Beg, request, supplicate for, *v.*	Phî.	
Behind, afterwards, subsequent to, later than, *prep.* and *adv.*	Ning-dim'î.	
Belch, *v.*	Kâ'ok.	
Believe, *v.*	Yûm.	
Belly, stomach, *n.*	Kan.	
Below, in a lower place.	Ka-tâ'î.	
Bend, crook, *v.*	Ma'gô dî.	"Dî"=do.
Bend, in river, road, &c., &c., *n.*	Phûng'gâ.	
Besides, over and above, in addition, furthermore, *adv.*	Dai n'thom'î.	
Be quiet.	Tem'di ngâ.	Compound verb, *vide* page 42 of grammar.
Bhat (cooked rice), *n.*	Shat.	
Bheel, *n.*	Kâ'nông *or* nông'khâ.	
Bind, tie, fasten, &c., *v.*	Khâng *or* sî'jup (tsî'jû).	
Bird, *n.*	Wû.	
Bite, *v.*	Wâ.	
Bitter, *a.*	Khâ.	Very long "â."

English.	Singpho.	Remarks.
Black, *a.*	Châng.	
Bladder (urinary), *n.*	Shi'bông.	
Blight, wither, shrivel, *n.*	N'san.	Assamese "pa'thân."
Blind, *a.*	Mî'pai.	
Blood, *n.*	Sai.	
Blow, fire, *v.*	Wan mût.	A [illegible] light fire.
Board, *n.*	Phûn pen.	
Boat, *n.*	Lî.	"Î" shorter than one in word for heavy.
„ bow of	Lî'bông.	"Bông"=head.
„ stern of	Lî'mai.	"Mai"=tail.
„ side of	Lâ-ma'kûm.	
„ bottom of	Lî'nêp.	
Body, *n,*	Khûm.	No perceptible difference in the sound of this word and the prohibitive particle "khûm."
Boil (make warm) *v.*	Sî'lûm *or* tsî'lûm.	
Bone, *n.*	N'râng.	
Bore, perforate, *v.*	Wâ.	
Borrow, take or receive as a loan, *v.*	Khâ.	
Both, the two, *a.* and *pron.*	Yon.	
Bough, *n.*	Phûn la'kûng.	"La'kûng"=largish, and "lá'kin" small branches.
Bow, *n.*	Kâ'lî n'dan.	
Cross-bow, *n.*	N'dan.	
Bowels, *n.*	Pû'kan.	
Boy, *n.*	Lâ'shâmâng.	*Lit.* male child.
Box, *n.*	Dêk.	
Bracelet, *n.*	La'khon.	
Brain, *n.*	Nû.	
Brass, *n.*	Ma'gî.	
Break.	No general word.	"Dût" (I can detect no difference in the pronunciation of this word, and the one for sell) means to divide, cane, string, &c. By violence "dô" means to break, or fracture.
Break wind, *v.*	Phet bû.	
Breast, also milk, *n.*	Chû.	
Bridge.	Ma'krai.	
Bring, convey, *v.*	Nôn.	*See* "Take."

English.	Singpho.	Remarks.
Broad, spacious, roomy, &c., *a.*	Ga-ba'.	
Broom, *n.*	Dûn'rê.	The verb is made by repeating the "rê," as "dûn'rê ve'û=sweep.
Brother, elder, *n.*	Phû.	
Brother, younger, *n.*	Nau.	
Brother-in-law, *n.*	Khau.	
Buffalo, tame, *n.*	Ngâ.	Very long "â."
Buffalo, wild, *n.*	Ngâ kai'khê.	"Kai'khê" is only used for a *wild* buffalo.
Build, or erect, house, *v.*	N'tâ gâp.	
Bullet, *n.*	Jê *or* uk'châ.	
Bull, *n.*	Kin'sû'ngâu.	
Bullock (castrated bull), *n.*	Kin'sû sû'dôn.	"Dôn"=root of verb, meaning to injure testicles by crushing them.
Burn, injure by fire, *v.*	Wan'î jû *or* tsî'khât.	
Burn, destroy by fire, *v.*	Nat *or* tsî'khât.	
Burn, as a fire, *v.*	Wan'tû.	
Bury, cover up, inter, *v.*	Lûp.	
Busy, occupied, *a.*	N'rau.	
Buttock, hip, haunch, *n.*	Ma'gî.	
Butterfly, *n.*	Lû'têp.	
Buy, *v.*	Ma'rî.	
By and by, before long, presently, *adv.* and *prep.*	Yet.	"Yet" usually indicates a near future time, though quite indefinite.
Calf, of leg, *n.*	La'bop.	
Call, bid, summon, invite, *v.*	Sî'gâ *or* tsî'gâ.	
Cane, *n.*	Rî.	
Caoutchouc (rubber), *n.*	Ko'noi.	
Capable, quick, useful, *a.*	Thap.	Only applicable to human beings.
Carry, in arms, *v.*	Pôn lâ.	Compound verb "pôn"=lift, "lâ"=take.
Carry, on shoulder, *v.*	Phai.	
Castrate, *v.*	Dôn *or* dân.	"Dôn" means to deprive of testicles by crushing process.
Cat, *n.*	Ning'yau.	
Catarrh, *n.*	Wâ'lû.	

English.	Singpho.	Remarks.
Caste, tribesman, race, *n.*	Phan.	Khi ma'khai He what phan tribesman? — What tribesman is he?
Catch, lay hold of, grasp, seize, capture, *v.*	Ga'rim.	
Catch fish, *v.*	Ngâ'gui.	
Cause, *i.e.*, effect by agency, power, or influence.	Sî'nûn *or* tsî'nûn.	It also means *empower, authorise, give authority to*, &c., &c.
Centipede, *n.*	Dûm'brâ.	Dûm-brâ'î* Centipede nâng'hâ stung. — A centipede has stung me.
Certainly, assuredly, *adv.*	Sing'dî.	
Change, alter, vary, *v.*	Ga'lai.	Substitute another thing for.
Charge, as a wounded animal, *v.*	Drû *or* thim.	
"Chang," raised platform, *n.*	Pan'râng.	
Cheek, *n.*	Sî'bî.	
"Chapuri" (open grassy plain).	Dan.	
Chest, *n.*	Sin'dâ.	
Chew, *n.*	Mî'â.	
Child, *n.*	Mâng	"Ka'shâ" is likewise used, though usually applied to the young of an animal.
Chillie, *n.*	N'prik.	
Chin, *n.*	Ning'khâ.	
"Chudder," cloth worn by women *n.*	M'bâ pai.	
Cinder (wood), *n.*	Wan gâ	
Clean (cooking pots), &c., *v.*	Ka'shin.	
Cleft, of wood, *n.*	Chen.	
Climb, mount, ascend, *v.*	Lûng.	
Cloth, *n.*	M'bâ.	
Cloud, *n.*	Mû.	
Cloudy, *n.*	Mû'khûp.	
Coal, *n.*	Gâ kâ'chang.	
Coat, *n.*	Pa'lông.	

* Nominatival "î," denoting agent.

English.	Singpho.	Remarks.
Coarse, thick, dense, close, crowded, &c., &c., *a.*	That.	
Cobweb, *n.*	Kâng'bâ chip.	
Cockcroach, *n.*	Si'lip.	
Cold, not warm, *a.*	Ka'shûng.	
Cold season, *n.*	Ning-shûng'tâ, *or* ma'ûn sî.	"Ning"=year, "tâ" from "sî'tâ"=moon.
Collect, scrape together, muster, &c., *v.*	Shûm'pûm, *or* tsî-khûm.	
Comb, *n.*	Pa'sî.	"Î" shorter than in word for cotton.
Comb, hair, *v.*	Bong ma'sit.	
Come, proceed, &c., *v.*	Sâ.	"Sâ" means to move from one place to another, hence it is used to express both come and go.
Companion, associate, comrade, *n.*	Nûm-nâng'wa.	
Complainant, *n.*	Drâ'dai sing'pho.	Participial construction, meaning man *who* complains. The "dai" is equivalent to our relative pronoun.
Consume, use up, finish (food), *v.*	Mâ	
Converse, talk with, *v.*	Ma'tâng.	
Cook food, *v.*	Sî'dû *or* tsî'dû.	
Cooking pot (earthen) *n.*	N'dî.	
Cool, moderately cold, *a*	Ka'sî *or* ka'tsî.	Very long "î," whereas the one in the word for *small* is shorter.
Copulate, *v.*	Krûm.	
Corpse, dead body generally, *n.*	Mang.	The word "sî"=die, dead, is usually prefixed to it.
Correct, precise, *a.*	Krak.	
Cotton (cultivated), *n.*	Pa'sî.	"Î" longer than in word for comb.
Cotton (from cotton-tree), *n.*	Ga'dûng pa'sî.	"Ga'dûng" = cotton (simol) tree.
Count, enumerate, *v.*	Tâk *or* rû.	
Country, *n.*	Mûng.	
Cover, overspread, *v.*	Mo'gâp.	
Cousin, *n.*	....	Same as brother.

English.	Singpho.	Remarks.
Cow, cattle, *n.*	Kin'sû *or* ken'sû.	
Coward, *n.*	Krit-da'wâ.	*Lit.* one who fears, *vide* note opposite "complainant." The "dai" has been shortened to "da" here for the sake of euphony.
Crank, used in a nautical sense, *a.*	Ka'prau.	
Crack, split, burst, &c., *v.*	Gâ.	Uttered sharply.
Crest, *n.*	(Wû) ning'tî.	
Cross, river, *v.*	(Khâ) rap.	
Crooked, bent, winding; not straight, *p. a.*	Ma'gô.	"Gô" uttered sharply.
Crow, *n.*	Kho'khâ.	
Crow, as a cock, *v.*	Wû goi.	
Cry, *v.*	Krap.	
Cubit, *n.*	La'dông.	
Cucumber, *n.*	Gûm'gin.	
Cultivate, *i.e.*, prepare land for crop, *v.*	No general word.	"Oui khen" = clear field of jungle, "phûn zat" = strip or cut off branches of such trees as have been felled, "oui nat"= burn (set fire to) jungle, &c.
Cunning, wily, *a.*	Zai.	
Cup (wooden), *n.*	N'khâ.	
Cure, restore to health, *v.*	Sî'mai *or* tsî'mai.	
Current, *n.*	(Khâ) phûng'ren.	
Custom, habit, usage, *n.*	Thûng *or* lai.	
Cut, with axe, knife, &c., *v.*	Ka'tham.	"Phûng lâng"= fell tree with axe.
Cut, hair, *v.*	Thou *or* ga'doi.	The Singphos don't cut their hair, but "thou," which means *lit.* to ring a tree, is used to describe the sort of hair cutting in vogue in these parts.
Cut, jungle, thatching-grass, &c., *v.*	Dan *or* dat.	Cut with sickle="mû."
Court-house, *n.*	Rûng n'tâ.	
Cymbal, *n.*	Shûp thêng.	"Dûm" = play same.
Dance, *v.*	Ma'nau.	

English.	Singpho.	Remarks.
Dark, not light, want of light, *a.*	Ning'shin *or* ning' tsin.	"Ning'shin shin'hâ," It is dark.
Daughter, *n.*	Nûm'shâ mâng.	*Lit.* female child.
Daughter-in-law, *n.*	Nâm.	
Dawn (early morning), *n.*	Ma'nâp.	
Day, period from dawn to darkness, *n.*	Ching'nî.	
To-day.	Dai'nî.	
Daylight, *n.*	Ning'thoi.	"Ning'thoi thoi'hâ," It is daylight.
Daily, *adv.*	Li-nî'mê.	
"Dao," *n.*	N'thû.	
Deaf, *a.*	Nâ phâng.	"Nâ" = ear.
Dear, bearing high price, *a.*	Ma'nû jâ.	"Ma'nu" = price, "jâ" (uttered sharply) = hard, here excessive.
Debt, *n.*	Khâ.	"â" very long.
Debtor, *n.*	Khâ ngâ'dai sing' pho.	*Vide* note opposite "Complainant."
Decay, rot, *v.*	Châm.	
Deceive, hoodwink, impose upon, *v.*	Lau.	
Deep, water, *a.*	Shûng.	
Deer, flesh, *n.*	Shan *or* tsan.	
Descend, go down, come down, dismount, *v.*	Yû.	
Desire, crave, want, express wish for, *v.*	Mit *or* mî'yû.	
Dew, *n.*	Nûm'rî.	
Dhan (paddy) *n.*	Mâm.	"Mâm sû'kong" = ear of ditto.
Dho'ti, loin-cloth, *n.*	M'ba bû	
Die, perish, lose life, *v.*	Sî.	
Dig, turn over earth, excavate, *v.*	Thû.	
Different, distinct, unlike, dissimilar, *a.*	Ga-gâ'.	
Difficult, *a.*	La-jâ'.	
Direction, of motion or progress, *n.*	Ma'gâ.	
Dirty, foul, nasty, soiled, *a.*	"Ga'grî *or* gû'grî."	Ga'grî kâp = soiled, &c.
Dismiss, turn off, send away, *v.*	Sî'dên.	
Disbelieve, *v.*	N'yûm.	
Distribute, divide, *v.*	Gam.	

English.	Singpho.	Remarks.
Ditch, hole, *n.*	Ga'dô.	"Dô" uttered sharply.
Dive, *v.*	Phûng'lip.	
Diver, *n.*	Phung-lip'da"wâ.	*Vide* note opposite "Coward."
Do, perform as an action, effect, &c., *v.*	Dî *or* dô.	
Dog, *n.*	Gui.	
Door, *n.*	Ching'khâ.	
Down stream, *n.*	Khâ'nam.	Usually used with "mo'-gâ"=place, toward, in direction of, &c.
Up ditto *n.*	Khâ'khû.	
Dove, *n.*	Kû'krû.	
Dowry, reward paid for a wife, *n.*	Khûm'phû.	Assamese "gâ'dhon."
Dream, *v.*	Yûp mâng mû.	"Yûp"=sleep, "mû"=see.
Drift, be floated away by current, *v.*	Chot.	
Drink, *v.*	Lû.	
Drinkable, suitable for drink, *a.*	Lû phâ rê.	"Phâ"=fit, "rê" affirmative particle.
Drive away, cattle, *v.*	Gau.	
Drown, *v.*	No word.	Sing'pho n'dai khâ'î sî'hâ (Man this water in died.) This man was drowned (died in the water).
Drum, *n.*	Thong.	
Drunk, *a.*	Cha-rû'î nâng.	"Cha-rû'î=liquor, "mod," with nominatival "î," denoting agent, attached.
Dry, *v.*	Sî'krâ *or* tsî' krâ.	
Duck, *n.*	Kai'pet.	Khampti word, "kai" means a fowl in Khampti.
Dumb, *a.*	Mâ'â.	
Dung, excrement, *n.*	Khî.	Uttered sharply. The "î" in "khî"=he is longer.
Dust, *n.*	Sû'mût *or* kûm'-pûn.	
Dwarf, *n.*	Chi'tât.	
Dwell, reside, *v.*	Ngâ.	
Each, every, *a.*	made by suffix "mê."	

English.	Singpho.	Remarks.
Ear, *n.*	Nâ.	"Á" very long.
Ear (to form ears), *v.*	Ga'jot.	
Earring, *n.*	La'kan.	
Earth, *n.*	N'gâ.	
Earthquake, *n.*	Dûm'shûm.	
East, *n.*	Jân prû ma'gâ.	*Lit.* spot, or direction, where sun rises.
Easy (not difficult), *a.*	N'la'jâ.	
Eat, *v.*	Shâ.	
Eatable, fit to be eaten, *a.*	Shâ phâ rê.	See note opposite "Drinkable."
Eave of house, *n.*	Boi'mûng.	
Echo, *n.*	Gâ phûng'tâng.	Gâ.
Edge, any sharp terminating border, *n.*	Ning'shan.	
Egg, *n.*	Wû'dî.	
Eight, *a.*	Ma'sat.	
Either, *conj.*	Made by a participle or by the conj. "kûn."	
Elbow, *n.*		
Elder, or eldest, *n.*	Lât.	
Elephant, *n.*	Mo'gui.	
Emerge, come or go forth, set out, appear, *v.*	Prû.	
Empty, void, unfilled, *a.*	Gû'man.	
Enciente (with child).	Mâng gông.	Only applied to human beings. Ken'sû n'dai / Cow this / nâ-sî'hâ. / pregnant. — This cow is with calf.
Enemy, foe, adversary, *n.*	Gûn'jan.	
Enter, go into, on, fit, set, decline, &c., *v.*	Shâng.	
Entirely, wholly, *adv.*	Song.	
Equal, equivalent, proportionate, adequate, *a.*	Ram.	Also of the same extent, measure, or degree.
Even, level, *a.*	Râ.	
Evening, *n.*	Jân'dû.	*Lit.* sunset.
Everday, *adv.*	Li-nî'mê	
Everywhere, *adv.*	Shî'râ yong goi.	*Lit.* places all in.
Explain, give explanation, *v.*	Sû yâ.	"Sû"=speak, "yâ"=give.

English.	Singpho.	Remarks.
Extinguish, *v.*	Wan sat, *or* sî'mit, *or* tsî'mit.	"Wan sat"=*lit.* kill fire.
Eye, *n.*	Mî	Uttered sharply.
Eyebrow, *n.*	Mî kôm mûn.	"Mûn"=hair.
Eye-lash, *n.*	Mî shû mûn.	
Eye-lid, *n.*	Mî kôm phî.	"Phî"=skin.
Face, *n.*	Man.	
Fall, drop, &c., *v.*	Krat.	
Fall from upright position, *v.*	Ga'dâng.	
Fall, slip accidentally, *v.*	Ka'tông *or* tông.	Mâng Child ka-tông'hâ. fell. } The child fell.
False, untrue, mendacious, *a.*	Ma'sû.	
Far, remote, distant, &c., *a.*	Sân *or* chân.	
Fasten, *v.*	Gît.	
Fat, not lean, *a.*	Phûm *or* sau.	"Phûm"=fleshy, plump. "sau"=oily, &c.
Father, *n.*	Wâ.	
Father-in-law, *n.*	Châ.	
Fathom, *n.*	La'lâm.	
Fear, fright, *n.*	Krit.	
Feasible, practicable, &c., *a.*	Mai.	
Feather, *n.*	(Wu) mûn.	"Wû"=bird.
Feel, have a sense of, *v.*	Dûm.	
Female, human being, *n.*	Nûm'shâ.	
Female organ, *n.*	Cha'khû.	No perceptible difference in pronunciation of this word and one for nine.
Fence, or bamboo enclosure, *n.*	Wâ krêng.	From "kû'wâ"=bamboo, "m'phân"=
Fetch, go and bring, *v.*	Sâ'lâ.	"Sâ"=go, "lâ"=take, &c.
Few, small in number, *a.*	Lo-î'mâ.	
Field, tilled land, *n.*	Oui *or* vî.	
Fig, *n.*	Ma-lû'sî.	
Fight, fisticuffs, *v.*	Ga'dûp.	
Fill up, make full, *v.*	Tûp dî.	Compound verb "dî"=do.
Fill in, load, *v.*	Bâng.	
Fill up or close a hole, *v.*	Pît.	
Fin, *n.*	Ngâ sing'không.	*Lit.* fish wing.
Find, come upon by seeking, *v.*	Tam lû.	Compound verb "tam"= seek, "lû"=get.

English.	Singpho.	Remarks.
Find, light upon, come upon accidentally.	Thâ'lû.	"Thâ" uttered sharply.
Finger, *n.*	Lî'ûng.	"Lî'ûng la'mî" = finger joints.
Finish, accomplish, complete, perform, *v.*	Thûm *or* ngût.	
Fire, *n.*	Wan.	
Fire-place, *n.*	Wan mâng.	
Fire gun, &c., *v.*	Gâp.	
Firefly, *n.*	Ken'thî thâng *or* n'thî thâng.	
Fish, *n.*	Ngâ shan.	"Shêp"= scale of ditto.
Fish-hook, *n.*	Mêk.	
Fishing-line, *n.*	Mêk sing'rî.	
Five, *a.*	Ma'ngâ.	
Fifteen, *a.*	Tsî ma'ngâ.	
Flame, *n.*	Wan lî.	
Flat, having an even and horizontal surface, *a.*	Chî'pen.	
Flea, *n.*	Wä si'lâng.	
Flesh, meat, animal food, *n.*	Shan *or* tsan.	
Flint, *n.*	Lûng jâ.	*Lit.* hard stone.
Do. stricker, *n.*	Wanpai.	
Float, *v.*	Wâ.	
Floor, bamboo, of house, *n.*	Pan'râng.	"Chang."
Flow, as a river, *v.*	Yông.	
Flower, *n.*	Si'ban.	
Fly, *n.*	Chi'krâ.	
Fly, *v.*	Pên.	
Foam, froth, *n.*	Bôp.	
Fog, *n.*	Sû'mui.	
Follow, go in pursuit of, pursue, chase, track, *v.*	Khân.	
Food, eatables, *n.*	Shâ phârai.	
Fool, *n.*	Ma'nâ.	
Foot, *n.*	La'gông la'phân.	
For, *prep.*	A'jo.	
Forbid, prohibit, *v.*	Khûm *or* phûng.	First most emphatic.
Forget, negligence, inattention, *v.*	Ma'lâp.	
Force, exert or use do. *v.*	Ning'gûn dat.	"Ning'gûn" = force, strength.

English.	Singpho.	Remarks.
Forehead, *n.*	Ka'than.	
Foreigner, guest, stranger, *n.*	Ma'nam.	
Forest, *n.*	Ma'ling.	"Nam'tâ"= small wood.
Four, *a.*	Ma'lî.	
Fourteen, *a.*	Tsî-ma'lî.	
Fowl, *n.*	Same as "bird."	
Fresh, good, not stale, unseasoned, *a.*	Ka'shing.	
Friend.	Ching'khû or tsing'khû.	
Frighten, *v.*	Sî'krit, tsî'krit.	
Frog.	Shû.	Uttered sharply.
Front of house, *n.*	M'pan *or* n'dong.	
From, *prep.*	Nan.	
Fruit, seed, *n.*	Phûn'sî *or* nam'sî.	Phûn=tree, Nam=jungle, bush.
Full, filled up, *a.*	Phing *or* phin.	
Get up, rise, *v.*	Rât.	
Get upon, mount, *v.*	Jau *or* lûng.	
Get, procure, obtain, *v.*	Lû.	
Ginger, *n.*	Sî'nam.	
Girl, *n.*	Nûm'shâ mâng.	*Lit.*, female child, "sî'rî" or "sî'wî," "mâng" also means a female child.
Give, bestow, furnish, supply, *v.*	Yâ *or* jô.	"Jô" means to bestow without receiving any return.
Give back, return, *v.*	Baiyâ.	
Glad, pleased, *a.*	Ông.	
Go, travel, journey, *v.*	Sâ.	*See* note opposite "Come."
Go away (begone), *v.*	Vî'ên.	
Goat, *n.*	Bai'nam.	
God, *n.*	Phrâ.	"Phrâ" really means an idol, "sig'yâ" or "jausig'yâ" is the word for God.
Goitre, *n.*	Dû'bông.	"Dû"=neck, "bông"= root of verb to swell.
Gold, *n.*	Jâ.	Uttered sharply, "jâ"= hard, strong, has longer "â."
Gong, *n.*	Bau *or* pau.	
Good, *a.*	Ga-jâ'.	
Goose, *n.*	Kai'hân.	

English.	Singpho.	Remarks.
Granary, *n.*	Mâm'dûm.	
Grandchild, *n.*	Shû.	
Grandfather, *n.*	Chî.	
Granddaughter, *n.*	Sî'vî shû.	
Grandmother, *n.*	Duî.	
Grandson, *n.*	Sî'dang shû.	
Grasshopper, *n.*	Khâm'kû.	
Grave, *n.*	Lûp wâ.	
Grow, increase in size by a natural and organic process, *v.*	Prâ.	
Guide, *n.*	Lam mo-dûn'da" wâ.	"Lam = road, "modûn da"wâ = shower (one who shows), *vide* note opposite "Coward."
Gum, *n.*	Wâ'nin.	
Gun, *n.*	Si'nat.	
Gunpowder, *n.*	Yâm.	
Hail, *n.*	Ma'sin ma'râng.	
Hair of head, *n.*	Ka'râ.	
Hair of body, *n.*	Mûn.	
Half, portion, part, *n.*	Kau'mâ.	
Hand, palm of, *n.*	La'tâ la'phân.	"La'tâ sing'dû" = back of hand.
Handful, *n.*	La-pai'mâ.	A handful.
Handle, of knife, &c., *n.*	Ning'khû.	
Hang up, suspend, *v.*	Noi.	
Hard, strong, difficult to accomplish, &c., *a.*	Jâ.	Uttered sharply.
Harlot, *n.*	Mê'phrê.	Khamptî word "mé" means "a woman" in Khampti.
Harrow, *n.*	Phû.	
Hat, *n.*	Kû'gûp gû'gûp.	
Have, possess, own, re-remain, &c., *v.*	Ngâ.	
Hawk, *n,*	Ga'lâng.	
He, *pron.*	Khî.	
Head, *n.*	Bông.	
Headman of village, *n.*	A'ghî.	
Headache, *n.*	Bông ma'chî.	
Hear, give ear, *v.*	Nâng.	"Â" longer than one in "nâng" to accompany.
Heart, *n.*	Sî'lûm.	
Heavy (not light), *a.*	Lî.	
Heel, *n.*	La'thin.	
Help, aid, &c., *v.*	Gû'rûm.	
Hen, *n.*	Wû wî.	
Hence, *adv.*	Dai'nan.	

English.	Singpho.	Remarks.
Here, in this place or spot, &c., *adv.*	Nâng'goi.	
Hide, keep, or put out of sight, *v.*	La'gan.	
Hide, keep oneself out of sight behind something, *v.*	Sing'bin.	
High, *a.*	Châ.	
Hill, mountain, *n.*	Bûm.	"Û" like "*u*" in bull while the "*u*" in "bûm" =swell, is like the *oo* in boom.
Him, *pron.*	Khî'fê.	
Hip, *n.*		
Hire, for a time, *v.*	Shâp.	
Hit, strike, object aimed at, *v.*	Krâ.	
Hoe, *n.*	Lî'khâ *or* kho'jak.	
Hoe, *v.*	Lî'khâ chî.	
Hold, have capacity for, *v.*	Tâng.	
Hole, excavation, *n.*	Khû.	
Hollow, vacant, *a.*	Krâng.	
Honey, *n.*	La'gât khû.	
Honeycomb, *n.*	La'gât chip.	
Hoof, *n.*	La'krû.	
Horn, *n.*	Rûng *or* n'rûng.	
Horn, *toss*, *v.*	Rûng khot.	
Hornet, *n.*	Gat'shâng.	
Horse, *n.*	Gûm'râng.	
Hot, *v.*	Ka'thet *or* lûm.	"Ka'thet" means heat from sun or fire.
Hot season, *n.*	Ning-lûm'tâ.	
House, *n.*	N'tâ.	
How (in what manner), *adv.*	Gi-ning'dî.	
How many?	Ga-dê'?	Sometimes carelessly pronounced "la'châ."
Hundred, *a.*	La'tsâ.	
Hunger, *v.*	Kâ'sî.	*Lit.* male.
Husband, *n.*	Lâ.	
Husk of paddy, *n.*	Mâm pûng'khâ.	
Husk paddy, *v.*	Mâm thû.	
I, *pron.*	Ngai.	
Idle, indolent, *a.*	La'gôn.	"Khûn'khân," a Khampti word, also used.
Ill, bodily ailment generally, *a.*	Ma'chî.	
Immature, unseasoned, *a.*	Gûng lûng *or* ga' lûng.	
In, *prep.*	Made by particles "goi" and "ī".	

English.	Singpho.	Remarks.
Incompetent, useless, *a.*	N'thap.	
Incubate, *v.*	Wû'dî phûm.	"Wû'dî" = egg.
Indian-corn, *n.*	Kâ'phâ.	
Indigo, blue, *n.*	Khâm.	
Injury, that which wrongs, *n.*	Khâ.	"Â," very long.
Insect	La'tûng.	
Inside, *prep.* or *adv.*	Ta'gui.	
Ink, *n.*	Mak.	
Insufficient, inadequate, *a.*	N'lô.	Lô, uttered sharply.
Iron, *n.*	M'phrî.	
Itch, eruption, *n.*	Sûm'bram.	
Itch, *v.*	Gî'yâ.	
Ivory, *n.*	Mo'gui kông.	*Lit.*, elephant tusk.
Jackal, *n.*	N'gâ gui.	*Lit.*, earth dog.
Jack-fruit, *n.*	Ma'lâng sî.	
Jealous, *a.*	Mit'î jang.	
Juice, sap, *n.*	Khû.	
Jump, *v.*	Gân *or* la' gân.	
Jungle, vegetation, *n.*	Nam.	
Keep, detain, retain, *v.*	Rêm.	
Keep quiet, *v.*	Tem'dî ngâ.	
Kick, *v.*	Kin'dit or la'phrê.	
Do. as a horse, cow, &c., *v.*	La'khat.	
Kill, destroy, *v.*	Sat.	
King, *n.*	No word.	"Chau'phâ" means head of a clan and "jau" is equal to our sir.
Kiss, *v.*	Pûp.	
Knee, *n.*	La'phût.	
Kneel, *v.*	Phût dî.	
Knife-blade, *n.*	Ning'shî.	Ning'shî ning'khûng = handle. Ning'shî ning'shan = edge. Ning krûng = point.
Knot, *n.*	La'khit or ma'kit.	
Knot, *v.*	La'khit.	To which tense suffixes may be attached.
Know, recognise, *v.*	Chêng *or* choi.	"Mâ chêng" = who knows, Assamese "kî ja'no"!
Knuckle	No word.	
Ladder of bamboo, *n.*	La'kâng.	

English.	Singpho.	Remarks.
Labour, toil, work, *v.*	Mûng'lî di *or* rai.	"Rai" is one of the substantive verbs.
Lame, *a.*	La'bê.	
Land (in contradistinction to water), *n.*	Kông.	Ngai kong'î sâ'hâ / I land.by came { I came by land.
Land, low, *n.*	Khâ'rô n'gâ.	Hollows.
Large, big, great, bulky, *a.*	Ga-bâ'.	Also spacious, broad, wide, &c.
Language, *n.*	Gâ.	
Last, after all the rest, *a., adv.*	Ning-dim'î.	Also means later in time, afterwards.
Last year, *n.*	Ma'ning.	Sing-oi'î ning, also used.
Last month, *n.*	Sî'dai sî'tâ wâ *or* sî'tâ sîda'wâ.	*Vide* note opposite "Coward"
Laugh, *v.*	Ma'nî.	
Lay egg, *v.*	Wû'dî dî.	
Leach, *n.*	Wat.	
Leaf, *n.*	Lap.	
Leak, *v.*	Gî'yûm.	
Learn, give or receive instruction, *v.*	Sî'rin.	
Leave, quit, relinquish, desist, stop work, &c., *v.*	Yû.	Uttered sharply.
Leave, quit, depart, *v.*	Wâ.	"Wâ" has the sense of returning, or leaving a person or place.
Leg, *n.*	La'gông.	
Foreleg, of animal, *n.*	Ka'phâ la'gông.	Shoulder, or forequarter.
Hind ditto, *n.*	Ma'ghî ditto.	
Leisure, *n.*	Rau.	I can detect no difference in sound between this word, and the one for together.
Lemon, lime, *n.*	Si'lui m'prik.	"M'prik" means a chillie.
Leopard, *n.*	Rong'teng.	
Let, allow, permit, *v.*	Sû *or* ngû.	
Let go, suffer to go free, release, *v.*	Dat.	
Lick, *v.*	Ma'tâ.	
Lie down, *v.*	Tôn.	{ Khî tộng'dî ngâ dai, / He lying down is } He is lying down.
Lift, raise, *v.*	Pôn.	
Light, not heavy, *a.*	Châng.	

English.	Singpho.	Remarks.
Light, not dark, *a.*	Ning'thoi.	
Lightning, *n.*	Mû'phrâp.	
Like, similar, resembling, *a.*	Phâ *or* sot.	Shĭ-rong' nâ ning'gûp phâ. (Tiger's face like.) Like a tiger's face.
Lip, *n.*	Ning'then.	
Liquor (local), *n.*	Cha'rû.	Our liquor is called "lâ' hû."
Listen, *v.*	Ma'dât.	
Lime, for eating, *n.*	Ning'thûn.	
Load, burden, *v.*	Ma'gûn.	
Load gun, *v.*	Yâm bâng.	"Yâm" = powder.
Load boat, elephant, cart, &c., *v.*	Tâng.	
Loaded gun.	Yâm bâng'dai si'nat.	*Vide* note opposite "Complainant."
Loin-cloth, *n.*	Sing'jûp.	Really small flap of cloth worn over private parts by males.
Long, in length, extended, *a.*	Ga'lû.	
Look, direct attention to, examine, &c., *v.*	Yû.	
Lose, *v.*	Mât.	
Loom, *n.*	Da' lâng.	
Loose, not tight, *a.*	Ko'rô.	
Louse (head louse), *n.*	Bông chî.	
Louse, *v.*	Chî yû.	"Yû" = look for, "chî deu" = kill, do, between two thumb-nails.
Low, near the ground.	Nêm.	
Luck, *n.*	No word.	"Ka'than" (= forehead) "gajâ'" is equivalent to the Assamese "kô'pâl bâ'rô."
Maggot, *n.*	Bêt.	
Make, execute, produce, &c., *v.*	Sî'jô *or* tsî'jô.	
Male, human being, *n.*	Lâ'shâ.	
Man, person, *n.*	Sing'pho *or* tsin'pho.	
Male organ, *n.*	Ma'nê.	
Mango, *n.*	Mû'mûng.	
Many, numerous, *a.*	Tô *or* ât.	"Lô," uttered sharply.

English.	Singpho.	Remarks.
Mask, *n.*	Phi'phai.	*Lit.*, ghost, monster.
Master, *n.*	Nûm-dû'wâ.	
Mat, *n.*	Pa'nêp.	
Matter, that with regard to, or about which anything takes place.	Rê *or* rai.	"Ma' khai rai'hâ"? What happened? } What has happened?
Mature, as applied to crops, &c., seasoned, *a.*	Kûng'sâ.	
Measure, *v.*	Si'don.	
Medicine, *n.*	Chî *or* tsî.	Pronounced sharply.
Meet, fall in with one another, *v.*	Ka'tût *or* khrûm.	
Micturate, *v.*	Jit'jî.	
Midday, *n.*	Jân bûng ding.	
Middle, midst, *adv.*	Khâ-âng'î.	
Midnight, *n.*	Yûp'tûng.	Ning'shin khâ'âng. Night middle. } Also used.
Milk, *n.*	Chû.	Uttered sharply.
Mithon, tame, *n.*	Ngâ'pho.	"Pho," uttered sharply.
Ditto, wild, *n.*	Pho'lam.	
Mine, *pro.* and *a.*	Ngai'nâ *or* nyê'nâ.	
Mistake, blunder, error, fault.	N'chât.	
Miss, fail to hit, *v.*	N'krâ.	
Mistress, *n.*	Nûm'shâ nûm'dû *or* nûm-dû'jan.	
Mix, *v.*	Gi'yô *or* ga'jam.	
Money, *n.*	Kûm'phrông.	Really means silver.
Monkey, *n.*	Woi.	
Month, moon, *n.*	Si'tâ.	
Moon, full, *n.*	Si'tâ phûng'âng.	
Moon, new, *n.*	Si'tâ ning'nâm.	
Moonlight, *n.*	Si'tâ ning'thoi.	
More, other besides, *a.*	Jat *or* yâ'mang.	
Mosquito, *n.*	Chi'krong.	
Morrow, *n.*	M'phô'nî.	
Day after do, *n.*	Phrâng'nî.	
Mother, *n.*	Nû.	
Mother-in-law, *n.*	Nî.	
Motherless, orphan, *n*	Chi'krai.	*Lit.* orphan, "nû ka'tâ" = motherless.
Mouse, *n.*	Yû.	

English.	Singpho.	Remarks.
Moustache, *n.*	Nyeng mûn.	
Mouth, *n.*	Ning'gûp.	
Mouth of river, *n.*	(Khâ) ma'jûp.	
Much, great in quantity or amount, *adj, adv.*	Shî' ba *or* tsî'bâ.	Also means in a great or high degree.
Mud, *n.*	Kûm'pâ.	
Musk pod, *n.*	Hom'chîng.	
Must, physical, and moral necessity, *v.*	Râ.	"Râ," also means need, require.
Myself, *pron.*	Ngai / I. } ting'nâng.	
My, *pron.*	Nyê *or* ngai'nâ	
Nága (tribe on north-eastern frontier), *n.*	Kha'khâng, *or* khâng.	
Nail, finger, *n.*	Li'min.	
Nail, toe, *n.*	La'gông li'min.	La'gông = foot.
Naked, nude, *a.*	Lâ'kân.	
Name, *n.*	Ming.	
Narrow, not wide, *a.*	Kêp.	
Navel, *n.*	Chû'dai.	
Near (not remote), *adv.*	Nî *or* ma'son.	
Neck, *n.*	Dû.	Uttered sharply.
Necklace, *n.*	Mo'hâ ka'chî.	"Mo'hâ" = four-anna bit, "ka'chî" = bead.
Needle, *n.*	Sa'mit.	
Neither, *comp. pron.*	Made by using "mang" = and, the substantive verb "ngâ" in its negative form.	*Vide* grammar for examples.
Nest, *n.*	(Wû) chip, *or* tsip.	
Net, hand net, *n.*	Sim'gon.	
Never, at no time, *adv.*	Made by using "ga'loi mang" with a negative verb.	Ngai ga'loi mang n'sâ / I never not go. } I will never go.
New, not old, *a.*	Ning'nân.	
Night, dark, darkness, *n.*	Sî'nâ.	
To-night, *n.*	Dai'nâ.	
Morrow night, *n.*	M'phô'nâ.	
Last night, *n.*	Ma'nâ.	
Nine, *a.*	Cha'khû.	
Nineteen, *a.*	Tsî cha'khû.	

English.	Singpho.	Remarks.
Ninety, *a.*	Cha'khû tsî.	
Nipple, breast, *n.*	Chû'sî.	
No, not so.	N'rê.	
Noise, generally, *n.*	Shî'râ.	
Noise, of voices, wrangling, *n.*	Ma'rû.	
Nobody, *n.*	Da'mâ mang n'ngâ.	*Lit.*, who even exists not.
North, *n.*	N'dûng ma'gâ nâ'hong.	Khampti word also used.
Nose, *n.*	Nâ'dî.	
Nostril, *n.*	Nâ'dî khû.	"Khû" = hole.
Not.	Formed by prefixing negative particle "n" before verbs,' adjectives, &c	" N,sâ'hâ" = I did not go, "N'ga-jâ'" = not good.
Nothing	Phâ mang n'ngâ.	
Now, *adv.*	Yâ.	
Nowhere, *adv.*	Ga-dê'goi mang n'ngâ.	Uttered sharply.
Oath, *n.*	Dûm'lû.	"Dûm'lû kham." = take oath.
Oil, for eating, *n.*	Nâ'man.	
Oil, for lighting, *n.*	Nâ'min.	
Old, not new, *a.*	Ning'sâ.	
Old man, *n.*	Ding'lâ.	
Old woman, *n.*	Gûm'gai.	
On, *prep.*	Ning-shângî.	*See* above.
One, *num. a.*	Ai.	
Once, *adv.*	Ga-lâng'mâ.	
Only, *a.*	Chû.	
Open, unclose door, box, &c., *v.*	Phâ.	
Open (unconfined), space	Shi'râ chi'kan.	
Or, *conj.*	Kiûn.	
Orange, *n.*	No name.	
Order, command, *n.*	Á'khâng.	
Other, *pron.* and *a.*	Ga-gâ'.	" Yâ mang " also used.
Otter, *n.*	Sî'ram.	
Orphan, *n.*	Chi'krai.	Like the Assamese word, it means without either or both parents.
Our, *pron.*	Î' nâ.	
Outside, exterior, *n.*	Sing-gan'î.	Also means in addition to, besides.

English.	Singpho.	Remarks.
Overtake, came up with, &c., *v.*	Lîp.	
Own, *poss. pron.*	Ting-nâng'nâ.	
Owl, *n.*	Wû khû kûm'bau.	
Paddle, *n.*	Lî'sham.	
Paddle boat, *v.*	Lî sî'gâ, *or* tsî'gâ.	
Pair, two of a kind, *n.*	Pâng'mâ.	Only applicable to a pair of bullocks. "Gôp'mâ" = pair of bracelets, earrings, &c.
Palatable, to drink.	Lû mû.	
Ditto, to eat.	Shâ mû.	
Pân.	Bû lap.	"Lap"= leaf.
Pânjî.	Ma'sôn.	"Ma'sôn jûn"= fix ditto.
Paper	Jî lap.	
Parrot	Wû'gê.	
Party, batch, assembly, *n.*	Bok'mâ.	
Peacock, *n.*	Wû'tông.	
Peel, rind, skin, *n.*	Phî.	
Peel, strip off skin, *v.*	Phîgâ *or* ê'ên.	
Permit, allow, let, *v.*	Ngû or tsî'nûn.	
Perspiration, *n.*	Si'lat.	Ngai si'lat phá'hâ. } I perspired.
Pestle	Thû mûn.	"Thû" uttered sharply.
Petticoat.	M'bâ la'bû.	The word being used for both a male and female nether garment "nûm'shâ" or "lâ'shâ" must be prefixed to specify which is meant.
Picture	Ma'kâ.	
Pick, pluck, pull off, *v.*	Lap'dî.	
Pick up a thing, *v.*	Thâ.	
Piece, portion of any thing, *n.*	Dông.	
Pierce, with spear, arrow, ibullet, &c., *v.*	Ga'lûn.	"La'phrang" = pass through, as a spear, bullet, &c.
Pig, tame, *n.*	Wâ.	
Pig, wild, *n.*	Nam wâ.	"Nam"=jungle.
Pigeon, *n.*	Kâ'gê *or* gâ'gê.	
Pillow, *n.*	Bông khûm.	
Pinch, *v.*	Ma'thî.	
Pine-apple,	Wâ sing'nâ.	
Pipe, *n.*	Lû'dî.	
Pity, affection, kindness.	N'gâ.	"N'gâ" is nearer our word "kind" than any other.
Place, spot, site, locality, &c., *n.*	Shî'râ *or* tsîrâ.	

English.	Singpho.	Remarks.
Place, set, deposit, *v.*	Dâ.	
Plain, level, even flat, as applied to land, *a.*	Lí'yâng.	
Plank, *n.*	Phûn pen.	
Plant, *v.*	Khai.	
Plantain, *n.*	Lûng'û.	"Lang'â"=stem of do.
Plate, *n.*	Bân.	
Play (amusement), frolic as children, *v.*	Chai.	
Pocket, *n.*	M'phêng.	
Poison, *n.*	La'bû.	
Pole, used in boat, *n.*	Mai'thu *and* spam-thû.	
Plough, *n.*	Thai.	
Plough, *v.*	(Ngâ) thû.	"Ngâ"=buffalo.
Poon, salt lick, *n.*	Chî'it.	
Poor, indigent, *a.*	Ma'chan.	
Post, *n.*	Sî'dâ.	
Potato, *n.*	Nai.	
Pour out water, *v.*	N'chin jô.	"N'chin"=water.
Pour in ditto	" dat.	"N'chin"=water.
Pour away ditto	" khô.	"N'chin"=water.
Powder, *n.*	Yâm.	
Pretty, comely, fair (applied to human beings), *a.*	Phrâ'phrû.	"Shôp"=nice pleasing to the senses; as, that is a nice cloth.
Pull, draw, tug, drag, *v.*	Gâng.	
Puppy, *n.*	Gui ka'shâ.	
Pumpkin, *n.*	Kan'tau sî.	
Punkah, *n.*	La'wît *or* La'vît.	
Pull down, demolish house, *v.*	Rûn.	
Presently, by and by, *adv.*	Yet.	"Yet" means soon, by and by, but it is often used to mean any subsequent period from five minutes to several hours.
Push, *v.*	Ga'nông.	
Putrid, decomposed, *a.*	Yêt.	No difference in sound between this word and the one for soon, except that here the "e" should be long.

English.	Singpho.	Remarks.
Put on coat, *v.*	Phûn.	"Pa'lông phûn'û"* = put on coat.
" "pagri," *v.*	Bâm.	"Bâm'bam bâm'û"* = put on "pagri."
" bracelet, *v.*	Khon.	"La'khon khon'û"* = put on bracelet.
" earrings, *v.*	Kan.	"La'kan kan'û."
Prick with thorn, *v.*	Jû.	
Quarrel, *v.*	Ning'get.	
Quickly, *adv.*	Ga'lau.	
Quiver, *n.*	Pa'lâ n'dûm.	
Raft, *n.*	Wân.	
Rage, anger, passion, *n.*	Mi'sin pôt.	
Rain, *n.*	Ma'râng.	
Rainbow, *n.*	Tûn'gâ lâ'tûm.	
Rapid, *v.*	Lûng'rai.	"Lûng" = stone.
Rat, *n.*	Yû jûng.	
Raven, *n.*	Kô'khâ.	
Raw, green, unseasoned, *a.*	Ka'ching.	"N'khût" = uncooked, *see* "Fresh."
Read, *v.*	Phat.	
Really, in truth, *adv.*	Sing'dî.	
Reach (to touch by extending hand or by anything held in it) *v.*	Dêp.	
Reap grain, *v.*	Mû *or* rêp	
Rear, bring up young, *v.*	Rêm.	"Rêm" merely means to keep, take care of.
Receive, obtain, accept, take, *v.*	Lâ *or* lû.	
Recover, get or obtain again, *v.*	Bai'lû.	"Bai" appears to be equal to the English prefix *re*; as "bai'lâ" = retake, "bai'lû" = recover, bai'yâ = restore, &c.
Red, *a.*	Khêng.	
Repair, renew, mend, *v.*	Ga'brâ.	
Reprisal, *v.*	Ning-gûn'î lâ.	*Lit.*, force by take.
Remain, stay, wait, tarry *v.*	Kring.	
Remainder, balance, rest, *n.*	N'chen.	

* "û" Imperative suffix.

English.	Singpho.	Remarks.
Rescue, retake, recapture by force, *v.*	Ning-gûn'î bai'lâ.	*Lit.*, force by recover.
Resemble, to be like to, *v.*	Sot san.	
Reside, dwell, live, *v.*	Ngâ.	
Return, turn back (go or come again to same place), *v.*	Bai'wâ.	
Return, give back, carry or send back, *v.*	Bai'yâ bai dat.	
Revenue, *n.*	Pan'dâ.	
Rhinoceros, *n.*	Dûn.	
Rib, *n.*	Ga'rêp n'râng.	
Rice (husked paddy), *n.*	N'gû.	
Rice (unhusked) paddy, *n.*	Mâm.	
Rice, cooked, *n.*	Shat.	Also means victuals.
Rich, affluent, possessing property, *a.*	Chi'thê *or* sû.	
Ring, *v.*	Lâk'chop.	
Ring tree, *v.*	Thon.	
Ripe, *a.*	Min.	Same as Miri and Abor.
Rise, get up, *v.*	Rôt *or* rât.	
Rise, in river.	Tûng.	
Fall in do.	Khêt.	
River, *n.*	Khâ.	
Road, *n.*	Lam.	
Rod, *n.*	Mêk phûng'gûn.	
Roll, cause to revolve by turning over and over, *v.*	Ga'leng.	
Roof, thatch, *n.*	Sûng'û.	
Room, *n.*	N'dûn.	
Root of tree, &c., *n.*	Phûn rû.	
Rope, *n.*	Sing'rî.	
Rotten, *a.*	Phû, yêt.	The two words appear to be interchangeable.
Rough, not smooth, *a.*	Mo'zût.	
Round, *a.*	Gûm'din.	
Rub, *v.*	Ga'nûn.	
Rubber, *n.*	Ko'noi.	
Run, *v.*	La'gat.	
Run away, escape, *v.*	Phrong.	
Rust, *n.*	Lûng'khân.	
Rupee, *n.*	Da'lâ.	
Saddle, *n.*	Án'mâ.	
Salt, *n.*	Jûm.	

English.	Singpho.	Remarks.
Saltpetre, *n.*	Yâm ka'ching.	
Salute, greet, *v.*	Nâ.	
Same, of like kind, identical, *n.*	Ai'mâ sot *or* ai'mâ rê.	
Sand, *n.*	Kûm'sai.	
Sap, gum, *n.*	Phûn bê.	
Say, speak, affirm, *v.*	Sû.	
Scar, cicatrix, *n.*	Wan'ping.	"Wan'ping" scar from a burn.
	Ning'sam.	"Ning'sam" ditto cut.
Scold, chide, *v.*	Ngan.	
Scratch, as a cat, tiger, &c., *n.*	Ma'khrî.	
Scratch, as a human being for itch, &c., *v.*	Sî'kroi *or* tsî'kroi.	
Seduce, lead astray, *v.*	Ma-tâng'dî tsî' phrong.	*Lit.*, conversing with, cause to run away.
Seat, wooden, *n.*	La'khûm.	
See, perceive by the eye, *v.*	Mû.	"Dông" meaning distinguish, perceive, also used.
Seed, *n.*	Tûm.	
Seek, search for, *v.*	Tam.	
Seer, one who sees, *n.*	Mû-da'wâ.	*See* note opposite "Coward."
Seer, 2-lb. weight, *n.*	Dok.	
Seize, *v.*	*See* "Catch."	
Self, *n.*	Ting'nâng.	
Sell, *v.*	Dût.	
Send, messenger, &c., *v.*	Dat.	Also means release, let go.
Serviceable, useful, *a.*	Khô.	
Seven, *a.*	Sin'it.	
Seventeen, *a.*	Tsî sin'it.	
Seventy, *a.*	Sin'it tsî.	
Sew, *v.*	Chui.	
Shade, shadow, *n.*	Sing'nip.	
Shake, tree, *v.*	Gang'ât *or* ga'nôn.	
Shallow, not deep, *a.*	Tâng.	
Shame, *a.*	Gî'yâ.	
Share, *n.*	Man.	
Sharp, having thin edge, or sharp point, *a.*	Ma'dai.	
Sharpen, *v.*	Ga'rang	
Shield, *n.*	Ning'gâng.	
Shoot, *v.*	*See* "Fire gun."	
Shop, *n.*	Jê.	

English.	Singpho.	Remarks.
Short, not long, *a.*	Ka'tûn.	
Show, exhibit, *v.*	Mo'dûn.	
Shut door, &c., *v.*	Lâ.	
Shoulder, *n.*	Ka'phâ.	
Sick, *a.*	*See* "Ill."	
Silk, *n.*	Nai.	
Silk-worm, *n.*	Nai'rî la'tûng.	"Nai'ri" = silk thread, "lâ'tûng" = worm (silk).
Silver, *n.*	Kûm'phrong.	
Since, *adv.* and *prep.*	M'phrat.	
Sing, *v.*	Ning'kin *or* ning'-tsin.	
Singe, *v.*	Sî'khât *or* tsî khât.	
Sink, *v.*	Thin.	
Sister, *n.*	Nau*, same as brother.	
Sister-in-law, *n.*	Nam.	
Sit, *v.*	Dûng.	
Six, *a.*	Khrû.	
Sixteen, *a.*	Tsî khrû.	
Sixty, *a.*	Khrû tsî.	
Skin, *n.*	Phî.	Uttered sharply.
Skin, flay, *v.*	Phî gâ.	
Sky, *n.*	Mû.	
Slack water,	Kyâ.	
Slap, *v.*	Tim'phek.	
Slave, *n.*	Mî'yam.	

* "Nûm'shâ" or "lâ'shâ" = female or male, is prefaced to determine whether brother or sister is meant.

"Phu" means eldest brother only (Assamese "kokai") and so is not used for sister.

In every Singpho family the boys and girls are named according to seniority by a fixed rule, which is never altered or broken through, thus—

Boys.		*Girls.*	
1st boy is called ...	Gâm.	1st girl ...	Kâ.
2nd " " ...	Nông.	2nd " ...	Lû.
3rd " " ...	Lâ.	3rd " ...	Roi.
4th " " ...	Dû.	4th " ...	Thû.
5th " " ...	Tâng.	5th " ...	Kai.
6th " " ...	Yông.	6th " ...	Khâ.
7th " " ...	Khâ.	7th " ...	M'prî.
&c. &c.	&c.	&c.	

English.	Singpho.	Remarks.
Sleep, *v.*	Yûp.	Same in Miri and Abor.
Slippery, *a.*	Ma'nên.	
Slowly, *adv.*	Chau'sû.	
Small, not large, *a.*	Ka'chî *or* ka'tsî.	
Small-pox, *n.*	Mak.	Often pronounced as if there was an "r" between the "a" and "k".
Smell, *v.*	Ma'nam.	
Smoke, *n.*	(Wan) khût.	
Smoke pipe, *v.*	N'lût lû.	
Snag, *n.*	Khon.	Uttered sharply.
Snake, *n.*	La'pû.	
Sneeze, *v.*	Cha'thî *or* ka'thî.	
Snore, *v.*	Yûp'gok.	
Snot, *n.*	Nêp.	
Snow, *n.*	Gên.	
Soak, *v.*	Ching dâ.	
Soft (not hard), *a.*	Kî'yâ *or* kyâ.	
Sole of foot, *n.*	La'gông la'phân.	
Some, indefinite quantity, *a.*	Ai ai *or* kau kau.	
Somebody, *n.*	Da-mâ'mâ.	
Somehow (in some way), *adv.*	Gi'ning rai'dî mang.	
Something, *n.*	La'go'lâ.	
Sometimes, *adv.*	Ga-loi ga-loi'mê.	
Somewhere, *adv.*	Ga-dê'goi kûn.	
Son, *n.*	Lâ'shâ mâng.	*Lit.*, male child.
Sort, class, order, caste, *n.*	Phan.	
Sour, *a.*	Khrî.	
South, *n.*	N'dâ mâ'gâ.	Pai'jân.
Sow, *n.*	Wâ'wî *or* wâ'vî	
Sow (plant by strewing), *v.*	Gât.	
Span, *n.*	La'khâm.	
Span, *v.*	La'khâm khâm.	
Spark, *n.*	Wan yâm.	
Sparrow, *n.*	Wû châ.	
Spawn, *n.*	Ngâ'dî.	*Lit.*, fish-egg.
Speak, talk, utter words, *n.*	Gâ sîgâ *or* tsî'gâ.	
Spear, *n.*	Ning'rî.	Sing'kîn =throw ditto.
Spear *v.* (pierce), *v.*	Gálûn.	
Spectacles, *n.*	Mî'jet.	
Spider, *n.*	Kâng'bâ.	
" web, *n.*	Kâng'bâ chip *or* tsip.	

English.	Singpho.	Remarks.
Spin, *v.*	Rî rî.	
Spindle, *n.*	Khûng.	
Spine, *n.*	Mû'rûng n'râng.	
Spirit, sprite, *n.*	Nat.	
Spit, eject from mouth, *v.*	Mî'ên ma'thô.	
Spittle.	Mî'ên.	
Spleen, *n.*	Sâm'pai.	
Split, wood, *v.*	Gâ.	
Spoon (wooden), *n.*	La'kûng.	
Spread, mat, *v.*	Nêp.	
Sprout, germinate, *v.*	Tû.	
Squirrel, *n.*	Tû'khâ.	
Stand up, *v.*	Châp.	
Star, *n.*	Tsî'gan.	
Start (move suddenly from surprise).	Ga'jông.	
Stay, remain, tarry	Sî'lûng.	"Khring" also used.
Steal, *v.*	La'gû.	
Steel *n.*	Dân, *or* ning'jâ phri.	Hard iron.
Steep, *a.*	Ding' dûng.	
Step upon, *v.*	Ga'bê.	
Stepfather, *n.*	Wâ'doi.	
Stepmother, *n.*	Nû'doi.	
Stern, of boat, *n.*	Lî mai.	
Stick (cane) *n.*	Chong'wai	"Sing'doi," stick used by old people for support.
Stick, ground as a boat, *v.*	Châ.	
Sting, *n.*	Ma'len.	"Nâng," *v.* sting.
Stone, *n.*	N'lûng.	
Limestone, *n.*	N'lûng ning'thûn.	
Stool, *v.*	Khî ê.	
Stoop, *v.*	Gûm.	
Straight, not crooked, *a.*	Prêng *or* ding.	
Straw, paddy, stubble, *n.*	(Mâmoni) khû.	
Strangle, by hand, *v.*	Dû ma'nat.	"Dû"=neck.
Strangle, by rope, *v.*	Dû git.	*Lit.*, fasten neck.
Strike, *v.*	Dûp.	
Strong, spirit, liquor, *a.*	Hêng *or* jâ.	
Strong, possessed of strength, *a.*	Ning'gûn jâ.	
Stroll about, saunter, *v.*	Dâm.	
Substitute, *n.*	Ma'lai.	
Suck, *v.*	Chûp.	
Suffice, *v.*	Lô.	Uttered sharply, "ram" = equal, also used.

English.	Singpho.	Remarks.
Summer, hot season, *n.*	Ning-lûng'tâ.	
Sun, *n.*	Jân.	
Sunrise, *n.*	Jân prû.	
Sunset, *n.*	Jân shâng.	
Sunshine, *n.*	Jân mai.	
Swallow, *v.*	Mû'ût.	Mû-ût' û, swallow, phûng don't mî-â' û, chew. } Swallow, don't chew.
Swell, *v.*	Bûm.	The "u" in this word is much longer than the one in the word for hill."
Sweet, not sour, *a.*	Dui.	
Swift water, *a.*	Khâ jâ.	*Lit.*, river strong.
Swim,	Phûng yot.	
Sword, *n.*	Nâp.	
Taboo, *n.*	Nâ.	Uttered sharply, while the voice rests on the "â" in "nâ" = ear, to lengthen it.
Tail, *n.*	Mai'shan.	
Take, receive, *v.*	Lâ.	"Lâ" means to convey, move, so that it is used for bring as well as take, "nâ lâ'û"= bring it here, "thô'goi lâ'û" = take it there.
Take away, *v.*	Lâ'wâ.	
Take out, remove, *v.*	Shâ.	Uttered sharply.
Take off, clothes, bracelets, &c., &c., *v.*	Yân	"Rô," uttered sharply, also used; yân means more to untie.
Talk, converse, *v.*	Gâ ma'tâng.	
Taste food, *v.*	Shâ ma'dât.	
Taste liquids, *v.*	Lû ma'dât.	
Tattoo, *v.*	Thû.	Long û.
Tea, *n.*	Pha'lap.	
Teach, *v.*	*See* Learn.	
Tear, *n.*	Mî prui shî.	
Tear (separate by violence), *v.*	Jê.	
Tell, acquaint, bid, *v.*	Ngû.	

English.	Singpho.	Remarks.
Ten, *a.*	Shî *or* tsî.	
Tendon, *n.*	La'sâ.	
Testicle, *n.*	Nî'dî.	
That, *dem. pron.*	Sî'dai.	
Thatching-grass, *n.*	Khûn'dû.	
Them, *pron.*	Khî-nî'fê.	
Then, in that case, *conj.*	Dêng, *or* sî'dêng.	
Thence, from that place, *adv.*	Sî-dai'nan.	
There, *adv.*	Sî-dai'goi.	Little way off.
There, *adv.*	Ô-râ'goi.	Further off.
There, *adv.*	Thô'goi.	Some distance off. This latter word may be made to mean a very long way off by putting stress on the "thô."
Therefore, *adv.*	Dai'dî.	This is a participle, meaning, *lit.*, that being.
They, *pron.*	Khî'nî.	
Thick, close, crowded in space, *a.*	That.	
Thief, *n.*	La-gu'da"wâ.	*Vide* note opposite "Coward."
Thigh, *n.*	Ma'gî.	
Thin, not thick, *a.*	Phâ.	
Thin, not fat, *a.*	La'sî.	
Things, *n.*	Rai.	
Thirst, *n.*	Phâng ga'râ.	
Thirteen, *a.*	Shî ma'sûm.	
Thirty, *a.*	Dûm'shî.	
This, *dem. pron.*	N'dai.	
This much	N'dai thêng.	
That much	Sî'dai thêng.	
Thorn, *n.*	Jû.	
Thousand, *a.*	Hing'mâ.	
Thread, for weaving, *n.*	Rî.	
Threaten, menace, *v.*	Sî'krit, *or* tsî'krit.	
Throat, *n.*	Yû'krê.	"Krê" uttered sharply.
Throw, *v.*	Ga'mêng.	
Throw away, *v.*	Ma'gau.	
Thumb, *n.*	La'tâ la'nû.	
Thunder, *n.*	Mû sî'gâ, *or* tsî'gâ.	
Thus, in this, that manner, *adv.*	N'dai sot, sî'dai sot.	
Tick, *n.*	Wâ ma'grâ.	

English.	Singpho.	Remarks.
Tickle, *v.*	Gî'jok.	
Tie up, fasten *to a stake* a cow, boat, &c.	Gî'dûn.	
Tie, by twisting process, such as cane, *v.*	Si'jûp, *or* tsî'jûp.	
Tie (fasten generally), *v.*	Git.	
Tiger, *n.*	Sî'rông, *or* tsî' rông.	
Tighten, *v.*	Si'jâ (*or* tsî jâ) dî.	
Tight, not loose, *a.*	Chat.	
Tire, jade, &c., *v.*	Bâ.	Long "â", but word uttered sharply.
To, *prep.*	Made by particle "goi."	
Tobacco, for eating, *n.*	Yâ ûm.	
Toe, large, *n.*	La'gông la'nû.	
Toe, others, *n.*	La'gông lî'ûng.	"Lî'ûng"=finger.
Together, in company, *adv.*	Rau.	
Tongue, *n.*	Sing'let.	
Tooth, *n.*	Wâ.	Long "â." Mouth must be opened when pronouncing word.
Toothache, *n.*	Wâ ma'chî.	"Ma'chî" means any and all bodily ailment.
To-morrow, *adv.*	*See* "Morrow."	
Top, *n.*	Ka-lêng'gông.	
Torch, *n.*	Wan sî'nan.	
Touch, *v.*	Ma'grâ.	
Touch-wood, *n.*	Wan'mui.	
Town, *n.*	Tâp.	
Track, *v.*	Khân.	
Trade, *v.*	Pa'gâ gâ.	
Trader, *n.*	Pa-gâ'da"wâ.	*Vide* note opposite "Coward."
Transplant, *v.*	Thot'dî khai.	*Lit.*, pulling up plant.
Tree, *n.*	Phûn.	
Trouble, annoyance, *a.*	Jam'jau.	
Trunk of tree, *n.*	Ning'pot.	
Turn, make upper side lower, *v.*	Ga'lau.	
Turn over, upset overturn, *v.*	Khûp.	"Gî'vin"= turn round.
Turban, *n.*	Bông'bâm.	
Turtle, *n.*	Tau'bîn.	
Tusk, *n.*	Kông.	
Twelve, *a.*	Shî n'không.	
Twenty, *a.*	Khûn.	

English.	Singpho.	Remarks.
Twice, *adv.*	N'khong lâng *or* yâng.	
Twins, *n.*	Ma'rûn mâng.	
Two, *a.*	N'không.	
Ugly, not comely, *a.*	Phrâ n'phrû.	
Umbrella, *n.*	Chong.	
Unable, *v.*	N'ngût.	
Uncle, paternal, *n.*	{ Wâ'dî { Wâ'doi.	Father's eldest brother. ——— youngest do.
Uncle, maternal, *n.*	{ Châ. { Châ yût.	Mother's eldest brother. ——— youngest do.
Understand, *v.*	Chat.	"yut"=youngest.
Unfinished, *v.*	N'ngût.	Unperformed.
Unripe, *a.*	N'min.	
Unfasten, bundle, rope, cane, &c., *v.*	Yân *or* rô.	
Uproot, *v.*	Pê *or* bô.	
Unserviceable, *a.*	N'khô.	"Khô" uttered sharply.
Upstream, *adv.*	{ Khâ'khû. { la'thâ.	Locative particle "î" usually attached.
Urine, *n.*	Jit.	
Vegetable, *n.*	Sî.	
Vein, *n.*	Sai'lam.	*Lit.*, blood road.
Very well (used eliptically).	Ai yûm.	
Village, *n.*	Ma'rêng.	
Vomit, *v.*	M'phat.	
Vulture, *n.*	Lâng'dâng.	
Walk, *v.*	Lam sâ ngût.	*Lit.*, road go able.
Wall, of house, *n*	Si'gûm.	
Want, require, *v.*	Râ.	
War, *n.*	Phên.	"Phen khat"= make war.
Warm, *a.*	Lûm.	
Warm (make hot) *v.*	Sî'lûm *or* tsî'lûm.	
Wasp, *n.*	La'gât gâtjân.	
Wash, clothes, *v.*	Krût.	
Wash, face, *v.*	Ka'shin.	
Wash, hands, *v.*	Ka'shin *or* la'mit.	
Water, *n.*	N'chin.	
Wax, *n.*	Kûng'rêp.	
Weak, *a.*	Ning'gûn ka'tâ.	*Lit.*, without strength.
Weed, *n.*	Ching.	
Weed, *v.*	Ching bô *or* kên.	" Bô " means to uproot.
Weave, *v.*	Dâ dâ.	
Weigh, *v.*	Chên.	

English.	Singpho.	Remarks.
West, *n.*	Jân shâng.	
Wet, containing water, *a.*	Ma′dit.	
Wet, moisten with water, *v.*	Sî′phek *or* tsî′phet.	
Wet season, *n.*	Yû′nam.	
What? *Interrog.* and *rel. pron.*	Ma-khai′mâ.	
Whatever, *pron.*	Ma′khai rai′dî mang.	
When, at the time that, *adv.*	Made by participle yâng.	
When? (at what time), *adv.*	Ga-loi′mê.	
What sort or kind	Gi′ning rai′dai.	
Whence? *adv.*	Ga-dê′goi nan.	
Where? *adv.*	Ga-dê′goi.	
Which? *interrog. pron.*	Ga-dê′na″ wâ.	
Whistle, *v.*	U′gui *or* ka′phû.	
White, *a.*	Phrông.	
White ant, *n.*	Kû′khûn *or* gû′-gûn.	
Who? *Interrog. pron.*	Da′mâ.	
Whose?	Da-ma′nâ.	
Why?	Ma-khai′dî?	
Wide, *a.*	No word, ga-bâ′ =large, used.	
Widow, *n.*	Nûm′dû.	
Widower, *n.*	Lâ′dâ.	
Wife, *n.*	No word, nûm′shâ =female, woman, used.	
Wind, *n.*	M′bûng.	
Wink, eye	Mî grip.	
Winter, cold season, *n.*	Ning-shûng′tâ.	
Wing, *n.*	Sing′không.	
Wipe, *v.*	Ka′chût.	
Wish, long for, *v.*	Mit *or* mî′yû.	
With, means, instrument, association, *prep.*	Sî′râ (*or* tsî′râ) *or* da′phom.	
Without, destitute of, wanting, *prep.*	Ka′tâ.	
Woman, female, *n.*	Nûm′shâ.	
Womb, *n.*	Mâng rông′dai-m′phêng.	"M′phêng," pocket, bag, &c, *vide* note opposite.
Work, labour, *n.*	Mûng′lî.	
" " *v.*	Mûng′li di *or* rai.	

English.	Singpho.	Remarks.
Worm, earth, *n.*	Chû'kai.	
" intestinal, *n.*	Tûk.	
Wring, clothes, *v.*	Shûp.	
Wrist, *n.*	La'tâ la'mî.	Hand joint.
Write, *v.*	Kâ.	
Yam, *n.*	Nai'pho.	
Yawn, *v.*	Sî'khâm, *or* tsî'-khâm.	
Yes, *n.*	Li'ning.	
Yellow, *a.*	Chit.	
Yes, affirmation and consent, *adv.*	Rê.	
Yesterday, *n.*	Ma'nî.	
Day before yesterday, *n.*	Mâng'nî.	
Yet, up to present time, *adv.*	Yâ'mang.	*Lit.*, now even: "ga'lai" is likewise used.
Yoke, *n.*	Ning'krau.	
Yolk, *n.*	Di'tûm.	
Young, of animal, *n.*	Ka'shâ.	Also used to denote a child.
Young man, *n.*	Sha'brâng.	
Young woman, *n.*	Ma'khon.	"Sî'ri" is likewise used. It means a virgin, young woman.
Youngest, *a.*	Yût.	